WHY STARTUPS FAIL

AND HOW YOURS CAN SUCCEED

———————————

David Feinleib

Apress®

ISBN-13 (pbk): 978-1-4302-4140-9

ISBN-13 (electronic): 978-1-4302-4141-6

President and Publisher: Paul Manning
Lead Editor: Jeff Olson
Editorial Board: Steve Anglin, Mark Beckner, Ewan Buckingham, Gary Cornell, Morgan Ertel, Jonathan Gennick, Jonathan Hassell, Robert Hutchinson, Michelle Lowman, James Markham, Matthew Moodie, Jeff Olson, Jeffrey Pepper, Douglas Pundick, Ben Renow-Clarke, Dominic Shakeshaft, Gwenan Spearing, Matt Wade, Tom Welsh
Editorial Assistant: Rita Fernando
Copy Editor: Tiffany Taylor
Compositor: Apress Production
Indexer: SPi Global
Cover Designer: Anna Ishchenko

Distributed to the book trade worldwide by Springer Science+Business Media New York, 233 Spring Street, 6th Floor, New York, NY 10013. Phone 1-800-SPRINGER, fax (201) 348-4505, e-mail orders-ny@springer-sbm.com, or visit www.springeronline.com.

For information on translations, please e-mail rights@apress.com, or visit www.apress.com.

Apress and friends of ED books may be purchased in bulk for academic, corporate, or promotional use. eBook versions and licenses are also available for most titles. For more information, reference our Special Bulk Sales–eBook Licensing web page at www.apress.com/bulk-sales.

*To the entrepreneurs,
investors,
and friends
who made this book possible*

Contents

About the Author

David Feinleib is an investor, adviser, and serial entrepreneur. As an entrepreneur and venture investor, he has been responsible for investments totaling more than $100 million. His passion for entrepreneurship goes back to his childhood when he started writing and selling software programs at age 12. Feinleib later joined Microsoft, where he became the company's youngest technical evangelist. He started four companies between 2000 and 2005. One was acquired by Hewlett-Packard, another by Keynote Systems. After joining venture-capital firm Mohr Davidow in 2006, he became a general partner in 2009, where he led investments in consumer Internet and software companies. In 2011, Feinleib's love for entrepreneurship took him back to starting his own companies, while continuing to advise and invest in others. Feinleib holds a master's in business administration from the Stanford Graduate School of Business and a bachelor's degree from Cornell University, where he was a Kodak Scholar. He is also an avid triathlete and violinist.

Introduction

Some eight of ten new businesses fail within their first three years. Nine of ten venture-backed startups fail to generate meaningful returns. Venture capitalists turn down 99% of the pitches they see. The odds appear to be stacked against you!

But entrepreneurs often make the same avoidable mistakes over and over. *Why Startups Fail* can help you beat the odds and avoid the pitfalls and traps that lead to early startup death.

Numerous books have been written about winners like Apple, Google, and Facebook. Few, however, capture the mistakes: the key decisions that led to running out of cash and early startup failure. Some startups spend millions building products the market doesn't want, others spend too much too early on marketing and sales, and still others hang on too long without pivoting out of bad markets. Knowing how to avoid these mistakes doesn't guarantee startup success. But it certainly increases your chances.

Whether you are a soon-to-be entrepreneur thinking about taking the leap, a bootstrapped entrepreneur trying to energize a business three or four years in, or a venture-backed entrepreneur trying to scale, *Why Startups Fail* shows you the key mistakes that cause new ventures to fail—and how to avoid them.

As a serial entrepreneur and venture capitalist, I've been part of or witnessed a fair number of startup successes and failures, some of which you read about in this book. In some cases, I disguise the companies and players involved or use composites, but the essence of each story contains a powerful kernel of wisdom—or point of caution.

Most recently, I was a general partner at Mohr Davidow, a Sand Hill Road (Silicon Valley) venture capital firm with $2B under management, where I worked from 2006–2011. Before Mohr Davidow, I started four companies, two of which were acquired. I've bootstrapped and raised venture capital. I've experienced both sides of the fundraising process: raising money and investing it. I've bought and sold companies, and I worked at a big software company—Microsoft—in the 1990s.

Expanding on my popular VCDave.com blog post *Why Startups Fail*, I use short, powerful chapters to reveal the keys to successful entrepreneurship: excellent product-market fit, focus, superb execution, the ability to pivot, stellar teams, and wise spending. In *Why Startups Fail*, you learn from the mistakes I've seen made over and over and find out how to position your startup for success.

Market, Product, and Entrepreneur

Investors are fond of debating which they care about more: the market or the entrepreneur. Some argue that given a great market, they can replace the team in order to execute on and capture that market. Others invest in great teams.

The reality is, great entrepreneurs find great markets. They build world-class products for those markets. They create efficient organizations that can deliver those products to market—execution machines that outrun the competition.

What's more, many successful entrepreneurs are not necessarily first to market with their products. Rather, they build products that better meet the needs of their users.

In Chapter 1, I'll discuss how to avoid bad markets. We'll take a look at how some very successful companies pivoted from bad markets into good ones and how you can do the same.

No one sets out to build a bad product, yet it happens all the time. In Chapter 2 we'll talk about the reasons bad products happen to good entrepreneurs. I'll explain how you can avoid building products people don't want, reduce adoption friction, and gain rapid adoption.

Believe it or not, a lot of companies are missing an Entrepreneur with a Capital "E"—a market visionary and product picker. I'll talk about what to do if you've lost your edge as an Entrepreneur and how to get it back. We'll explore how to fail fast—since it's not failure itself that will kill your company but failing slowly that will do you in.

In Part 1, then, we explore three of the key ingredients for a successful start-up: a great market, a great product, and a world-class Entrepreneur. You'll come away with the knowledge to identify if any of these ingredients are missing—and how to remedy the situation.

CHAPTER 1

Poor Product-Market Fit

Pivot Your Way to a Successful Launch

It may seem obvious, but building a product the market wants is critical to keeping your startup from running out of cash. It's all too easy to keep your product in the back room, iterating on it for months or years, only to find out no one wants to use or buy it. Products the market doesn't want not only waste valuable capital, but also waste your time as an entrepreneur. Finding the right balance between customer feedback and staying true to your change-the-world vision is hard, but it's critical to all that follows: recruiting with a great team, raising capital, and selling your product.

Product-Market Fit

Many startups never achieve the elusive product-market fit. Once found, product-market fit transforms a startup's trajectory. Before a company finds product-market fit, nearly everything the company does (or should do) is about the search for product-market fit. After the company finds it, everything is about scaling: ramping up operations to accommodate a rising number of customers. You want to scale users/customers, team, and infrastructure.

Some companies—Facebook and Zynga, for example—find product-market fit right out of the gate. Or at least they appear to. Others, like Intuit, go along for years, sometimes teetering on the brink of bankruptcy, until they crack the code.

The best entrepreneurs are relentless in their pursuit of big markets and products to fit those markets. So why do so many startups never achieve the fit?

Some spend too much time on technology. They keep building without getting user or customer feedback. All too often, this happens with purely technical founders building product for product's sake. Some fear rejection: they take it personally when others don't want their product.

Others fail to face the reality of what the data tells them. They refuse to confront the tough questions: was my thesis incorrect? If so, what should I do?

Still more never find a way to reach their market. The market need is there, the product is compelling, but they can't reach their customers. Many companies trying to target the small-business segment have failed because of this. In such scenarios, a startup's success becomes a lot less about building great product and a lot more about efficiently reaching the potential customers.

But worst of all is achieving product-market fit only to discover that the actual market is very, very small.

Big Markets

Companies targeting small markets are more susceptible to failure than their big-market counterparts.

These companies can still be rewarding businesses—for a time. Some entrepreneurs don't have the aspiration to go after big markets or build big businesses, or they have a desire to build something small and boutique-like—a bed and breakfast, for example, or a local restaurant.

But when it comes to the most successful tech startups—Apple, Facebook, Google, Salesforce.com, to name just a few—great markets are synonymous with big markets. Companies with big markets benefit from economies of scale. They can spend more on customer acquisition and be more cost-effective on distribution, and, simply put, they have a lot more potential users of their product or customers to sell to. Amazon commoditized local booksellers; Walmart commoditized local retailers. Time and again, those going after big markets dominate those going after small ones.

As an entrepreneur, your goal is to find a big-market opportunity and deliver a product that captures it. Going after a big-market opportunity vastly reduces your chances of failure. To capture a big-market opportunity, you must start off with a *big market*.

No doubt that seems obvious, but I repeatedly see entrepreneurs start in small markets. It's just as hard to execute on a big-market opportunity as on a small one—sometimes harder. Yet entrepreneurs continue to target small markets. Why?

Often, big markets appear unassailable. For years, Electronic Arts (EA) dominated the software market for games. At one point, the company had a market cap of more than $17 billion. Yet in just a few years, Zynga, a new tech startup, swooped in and dominated a new area of gaming: social gaming. This was a market that EA should have dominated but failed to. That's because EA was trapped by its legacy model, whereas the founder of Zynga recognized a disruptive wave and seized it.

EA's games were expensive to produce. Its distribution model of putting software on retail-store shelves was both costly and outdated. It had to spend tens of millions of dollars on marketing to drive awareness of new games. Even for existing games, the company had to spend heavily on marketing to drive demand for new versions. And many of its games appealed only to a niche of hard-core gamers.

For all these reasons, many venture capitalists steered away from investments in the gaming market. They worried about the costs of content creation, marketing, and distribution. EA's competition came only in the form of other well-established players who could afford similar investments in development and distribution, such as Microsoft and Sony.

Ride the Wave

If you want to be a great surfer, you've got to find a great wave to ride.

Zynga founder Mark Pincus recognized that new social platform Facebook could provide an incredibly efficient way to deliver and market games. Zynga's social games used Facebook for initial distribution. They also incented existing users to get new users to play by making the participation of other users a core part of every game. In just one example, to build bigger and bigger cities in the Zynga game CityVille, users had to invite their friends to staff various functions in their city, such as the Town Hall.

Because they relied on lower-quality graphics, Zynga's games were far less costly to produce. Their relative simplicity and the fact that it was free to start playing made them appealing to a much broader audience. Zynga made sure there was zero friction to adoption: that is, nothing was standing in the way between them and their potential users.

Zynga stole what's called *timeshare*: it gave people an alternative place to spend their time during the day. Instead of consuming soap operas, they could now consume Zynga games and gain a sense of fulfillment—building a virtual city, for example—in the process.

The company also introduced innovative new adoption and monetization models. The games were free to play but required users to purchase virtual goods if they wanted to move up more quickly. Virtual goods were not a new concept—they had been available in Asia for years, and many skeptics of social gaming argued that such goods would never be adopted outside Asia.

But by making them easily accessible and a core part of the games, Zynga brought them to the mainstream. In part, this was because users felt they were getting the game for free to begin with, so they had less of an issue paying for items later. It was also possible because Zynga capitalized on social dynamics: players felt competitive pressure to buy virtual items that would help them win the friendly yet competitive games among their circle of friends. This coupled with addictive design and gameplay dynamics turned the games into cash machines.

Some of today's most successful tech startups have come about because their entrepreneurs recognized a market opportunity or disruptive wave and designed products to take advantage of those waves, introducing even greater disruption in the process. Zynga capitalized on the opportunity presented by Facebook and then introduced more disruption through low-cost games, new monetization models, and a zero barrier to adoption. Zynga is just one example of a company that was hugely successful in finding product-market fit in this manner.

Great Product, Bad Market

A talented investor once told me, "A great market and a bad product is better than a bad market and a great product." All too often, entrepreneurs target small markets. Although targeting a big market might seem close to impossible due to the gorillas already in that market, the reality is that attracting capital for businesses targeting small markets is a lot harder than raising capital to go after big-market opportunities.

Often, entrepreneurs are ahead of their time. Customers aren't ready to spend money on or change habits for unproven benefits. The company runs out of money waiting for the market to develop; or it tries to start over, but it's too late.

Company R (a composite) had a compelling concept, but customers weren't ready to buy in. CEO R proposed a restart: rather than sell to the market segment he was in, he would target a different market segment. As a result, he would significantly reduce Company's R's sales and marketing expenses. Company R was mildly successful with its new plan but burned through lots of cash before it reconfigured.

If you have a great team executing flawlessly, but there just aren't that many potential users or customers for your product, your team's potential is restricted. Many market opportunities simply aren't worthy of the teams that go after them. Conversely, teams that stick around in bad markets too long have to find out the hard way that the market always wins.

Product limitations can also restrict potential market size. Some products, for example, require significant customization and correspondingly high setup costs. That means it's expensive and time-consuming to extract value from them. Thus, the product becomes limited to those customers or users willing to make the time and capital investment to use the product—likely a lot smaller than the total market size originally envisioned for the product.

Company W had a product that should have appealed to the owner of every web site on the planet. But it took three to six months to customize the product and have it start working. Those customers willing to pay the price of implementation in both time and dollars saved tens of millions. Unfortunately, only a few were willing to make that kind of upfront investment, ruling out all but about 1,000 customers in the world.

The trickle-down effect was immense: the sales organization was structured for heavy, long-cycle selling. The product was designed to be customized, so getting to a self-serve model, although always a goal, never became a priority. When it came to sales, other companies couldn't compete directly on technology. But they came close by offering different solutions that solved the same problem. Those solutions weren't as effective, but they were good enough. Although the company had an incredible team, the true market—as restricted by the reality of the product—held them back.

Structural Issues

Some markets come with structural issues that can make achieving product-market fit extremely difficult. Life-science companies, for example, frequently face regulatory hurdles (for example, FDA compliance) that are specific to their market.

Markets like these often have existing monetization models—ways they turn their efforts into money—that companies must live within as well. When it comes to monetization, your users can pay, or a third party can pay you. Third parties can be advertisers, in the case of ad-supported businesses. Or they can be other large companies, such as healthcare insurers reimbursing patients for healthcare costs. One big mistake startups make is assuming people will pay when they won't.

It's very hard to change human behavior. That's especially true when it comes to trying to convince people to pay for something they're used to getting for free. Consider the case of healthcare startups. The widespread adoption of smartphones and iPads coupled with rapidly rising healthcare costs has encouraged many entrepreneurs to go after massive healthcare IT opportunities with innovative new software and hardware. Many assume that consumers will pay for these applications, yet consumers are used to employer-provided insurance covering their healthcare costs. As a result, these startups have to be extra savvy not only about finding the right product-market fit but also when navigating the structure of their market.

Finding Fit

As legendary entrepreneur Steve Blank once said, the best way to find product-market fit is to "get out of the building." Users and customers can't define your vision for you—nor should they—but they can inform it. Today you can get out of the building physically and go visit users or customers, or you can do it virtually.

Virtually getting out of the building can be as easy as putting up a landing page (that is, a one-page version of your product or service) and buying Google ads to drive traffic to it. Or you can release a beta of your product and drive organic growth.

It can mean building a version of your app and putting it in the app store to see if people will use it. It can also mean talking to customers and getting a few of them to commit to be early users of your product, if you build it.

Whatever your approach, these days there is no excuse for not getting out of the building. And certainly in the software world, there is no excuse for not pivoting repeatedly, and inexpensively, until you find product-market fit.

Reaching Your Market

Great product-market fit means having not only a product that matches the market, but also a way to distribute that product efficiently. As the old joke goes, you lose money on every sale, but you make it up in volume. Unfortunately, that model doesn't last long.

Small businesses have always been the siren song of target markets due to the immense number of them. But startups that go after small businesses find out the two painful truths of this market: the customers have little money and are very hard to reach.

When it comes to reaching customers, some markets hold you hostage. Company M, which was started long before Apple introduced the iPhone and Google introduced Android, had an innovative mobile product for consumers. However, the product had to be integrated with the wireless carriers (AT&T, Verizon, and so on) to work. Not only did the company have to negotiate business deals with the wireless carriers and get those carriers to certify its applications; it also had to develop, test, and integrate its software with every phone vendor on whose phone the software was to ship.

After several years, the company got its software deployed and started generating revenue for the carriers. Every time a phone shipped, the company made money. Then a not-so-funny thing happened: the carriers decided they didn't like the revenue split they had negotiated with the company, and they put a ceiling on the amount of revenue Company M could make. While still generating tens of millions of dollars in revenue, the lucrative contracts now had a limit. The company's revenue potential was restricted, as was its potential value.

The company had little recourse. The carriers controlled the distribution channel—each carrier had tens of millions of subscribers, and there was virtually no other way to reach them. The choice of target market limited the company's upside. "One thing's for sure—I'll never build a business like that again," the founder often said when asked about what he was going to do next.

Of course, partnering with big industry players that have existing distribution offers one huge advantage: you get to leverage their distribution. That works great as long as the value equation is relatively equal: your partners value your product, and you value their distribution. But if you end up with only one partner, or your partners can get a similar product somewhere else, watch out. You soon find your market holding you hostage.

When to Pivot and How

Changing direction is one of the biggest strategic decisions a founder ever has to make. Change course too early, and you never see an idea through long enough to understand whether the market will accept it. Wait too long, and you risk running out of cash. Change direction frequently, and you lose the confidence of your team and investors in your ability to lead. How then should an entrepreneur decide how and when to pivot?

Knowing when to pivot is what makes entrepreneurship an art and not a science. But the first step is to confront the data. Most entrepreneurs start with a thesis, whether they articulate it or not. They believe that if they build X, then Y will happen. More often than not, their thesis is incorrect.

The founder of Company B believed he could reach the market by signing up small businesses as customers and giving away the company's service for free to consumers. It turned out that the small businesses wanted the company to have millions of consumers using its service before they would sign on as customers. Although the founder eventually pivoted, it took him more than 24 months to make the change, wasting valuable time in the process. He went through multiple sales and marketing executives before admitting that although he was right about being in a big market ripe for disruption, his approach to taking his product to market simply wasn't going to work.

"What is the data telling me?" is critical question to ask yourself; being honest with yourself about the answer is even more so. When there is a difference between your thesis and the reality of the data, it's time to think hard about a pivot.

Data can make a potentially tough discussion with management, investors, and board members a lot easier. Although sunk cost logically shouldn't factor into what you do going forward, the reality is that sunk cost weighs heavily on both management's and investors' emotions when making decisions. Discussions about pivots may still be emotional and challenging, but when you use the data to frame them, they become a lot more productive.

Pivoting can be tough. But staying in a bad market is even tougher; and, ultimately, the market will eat up all your capital and beat you. Iteration is great for perfecting a product once there's demand, but more often than not, radical change is required—either in product or market—to achieve product-market fit.

Capitalizing Too Early

Raising too much capital too early can make pivoting even harder. The vast majority of investors prefer to invest in a strategy that's already working, when a company is at a key inflection point and needs capital to scale.

Some companies have to raise large amounts of capital even to have a shot at achieving product-market fit—those building hardware, for example. But outside of those companies, it's best not to raise too much capital until you've achieved product-market fit and are ready to scale.

Ironically, raising too much capital too early reduces your options more frequently than it expands them. Most investors expect companies to spend the money they raise in support of growth, not keep it for a rainy day. Whether they admit it or not, founders who raise a lot of money feel intense pressure to spend it.

Moreover, with big capital comes big expectations. The founder of Company E raised tens of millions of dollars based on his reputation as the former head of a very well-known tech company and the size of the market he was targeting. He marketed his deal exceptionally well and raised more than twice as much money than he had planned. He promised his new investors exceptional growth: growth that never came because he never achieved product-market fit. Thinking it was just a matter of getting the word out, he spent exorbitantly on marketing that never paid back with results, instead of focusing on product.

His competitor, Company C, came from behind and achieved ten times as much annual revenue in 24 months, starting from nothing. Company C ultimately became the market leader.

What did the two teams do differently? Company C's team focused ruthlessly on building just enough product to satisfy the company's target market, and then spent aggressively on sales and marketing once they saw that customers loved what they had built. In contrast, the founder of Company E painted a great vision, but having promised so much, never faced up to the fact that the market didn't want the product he'd built. After spending some $40 million, the company was recapitalized, and the investors brought in a new CEO to try to turn the company around.

Pivots That Worked

Many very successful companies started out doing one thing but had to change their target market in order to be successful. Microsoft began by building software-development tools but seized on the opportunity to sell the operating system software (DOS) that went with the new (at the time) personal computer IBM was introducing. In fact, Microsoft licensed the first version of the software from another company so it could ship the software.

Payments company PayPal started out as a service for beaming payments between Palm Pilots; it wasn't until the company focused on e-mail–based payments—and rode the huge wave of Internet auctions taking place on eBay—that the company became a runaway success.

Intuit was started in 1983, but it took years for the company to get significant traction in its market. The company teetered on the edge of bankruptcy before its marketing campaigns and the launch of Windows 3.0 made it successful.

In all three cases, although each company stayed true to its vision, each pivoted to capitalize on a large underlying wave.

Summary

Product-market fit is that often-elusive but critical success factor for every startup. Companies targeting big markets beat out those targeting small ones. Bad markets kill potentially great startups.

Failure comes from

- Starting with a small market
- Not confronting the data
- Holding onto an incorrect thesis too long

- Having to spend too much to reach your market
- Lack of an underlying wave

Market success comes from

- Going after a big market
- Building a product the market wants
- Pivoting until you reach product-market fit
- Efficiently reaching your market
- Riding a huge wave

CHAPTER 2

Bad Products

Less Is More

Many potentially great companies fail because they deliver bad products to market. Not because the product doesn't fit the market, but because the product doesn't work. It's hard to use, it breaks, or it doesn't do what the user thought it would.

To get people to buy or use something you've built, it has to be truly great. Large, established companies can get customers to buy bad products. But the tactics they use don't work for startups. Building a house of cards doesn't work either. Sure, you can spend a lot on sales and marketing to drive rapid customer adoption; but ultimately, those customers won't stick around, and neither will your company.

That's why customers and users have to love your product. Not only will they use it, but they'll get others to use it too.

No one sets out to build a bad product. So how do bad products end up getting built, and what can you do to make sure yours isn't one of them?

Falling Victim to Product Blindness

There is no substitute for building a product you love to use. When you use your own product, you experience first-hand the rough edges, the details, and the bugs that separate great products from bad ones.

Yet even those who use their own products deliver bad products to market. That's because everyone suffers from *product blindness*. Product blindness occurs when you use your product so much that you subconsciously work around the difficulties. Too hard to sign up? No problem—use an existing account for testing. Trouble finding your site on the Web? Not a big deal—you already know your site's address! Occasional data-reliability issues? Not an issue for your test account, because you just reload the data.

Using a product means *really* using it. Not for testing, not with test data or test accounts, but using it day to day. If you're building a game, that means actively playing the game, not just watching from the sidelines. If you're creating a product that serves businesses, it means running your own business using your product.

What should you do if you're not building a product you would use every day? Think twice about whether to build that product!

If you're still intent on building that product, either find at least one use case[1] in which you can use your own product, or partner with a customer to find that use case. Most often, this challenge arises in a business-to-business company that is building a product for other companies to use. Examples include applications such as HR, accounting, and inventory-tracking systems built for large organizations, as well as infrastructure products like storage systems. In these cases, it behooves you to build a key application you can use daily to test out the system, or to partner with a customer to build that application to address a key use case for them.

Consider the case of Company S (a composite), a storage company. The operations of the company weren't dissimilar from those of other startups— storing files such as customer presentations and product specifications. Yet the company was building a high-performance storage product for large amounts of data, intending for the product to be faster than any other on the market.

What did the company do? It partnered with a large customer that had years of data to work with.

Company S's engineers spent months working on-site in the customer's labs, using actual customer data to test the performance of the storage system. Members of the customer's team worked alongside Company S's engineers testing the product. Before the product was released to the broader market, Company S worked closely with the customer and a handful of other *early-adopter* customers to deploy the product in those customers' production environments.

---

[1] A *use case* describes a specific scenario in which a user uses a product. Ideally, use cases model an entire scenario end to end, including the outcome, actual user (what they do, who are they, and so on), and detailed steps in which that user interacts with the product.

It wasn't the same as every employee at Company S using the product daily, but it was a close second. As a result, when Company S delivered its products to market, they had already been tested in real customer environments.

Why did these customers agree to let Company S use their resources, which included space, infrastructure, data, and people? Because Company S created an *exclusive* early-adopter program, which provided access and discounted pricing to its upcoming product. But that alone wasn't enough. The real secret was that Company S was building a product that—if it worked—solved a very real pain point[2] for Company S's customers.

Had Company S's engineers built the product in the absence of the early-adopter customers, they would have become highly susceptible to product blindness. In comparison, the early adopters had no problem being incredibly blunt with Company S about key product issues. After all, they were consuming valuable time and resources working with the early versions of the product. The engineers at Company S fixed the product issues as a result.

How Bad Products Get Built

Now consider the case of Company T (also a composite). Company T spent years building incredible technology. The concept was powerful. Both investors and customers loved the promise of the product.

The reality, however, was another story. In practice, Company T's product failed to deliver on its promise. The product worked flawlessly for a very narrow set of use cases. But it didn't fare so well when faced with the breadth of use cases thrown at it by millions of users.

The company had unparalleled technology but couldn't make it accessible to users. The founder of Company T was an excellent technologist. He later said that he wished he had focused on real-world use cases sooner. Instead, like a moth to a flame, he was drawn to ever-newer innovations.

When the technology was 80% complete, for example, he moved on to the next problem. That by itself might not have been an issue—every organization needs forward-thinking technologists—but it set the tone for the rest of the

---

[2] *Pain point* is VC speak for the problem a product or a company successfully solves—usually something so painful that customers rush to buy the solution and make the startup successful.

organization that fit and finish weren't important. Unfortunately, customers thought they *were* important.

This is just one example of how bad products get built. To be fair, the 80% of the product that was built was incredible. It was the remaining 20% that failed. The products that Company T delivered never lived up to their promise.

Successful startups continually walk the fine line between delivering on the bleeding edge to get product into market, and sweating the details. Plus, it's no easy feat to stay focused on delivering great product while operating your business. Fit and finish require a lot of attention to detail. If you don't find those details interesting, hire or partner with someone who does.

Failure to Focus

As legendary football coach Nick Saban put it, the key to focus is to "eliminate the clutter."

One of the biggest challenges I see in venture-backed companies is a desire to build more-more-more. When companies are flush with capital, the hard tradeoffs are easier to avoid.

The same phenomenon occurs in many bootstrapped startups under the guise of not committing to a single strategy. It's good to change your strategy when it's not working. But you have to commit to a strategy first—even if only until you prove that it doesn't work. Some startups try so many different things in an incomplete way that they never truly get to test their product concept. Other startups simply don't have a clear vision of what they're trying to build.

The key to focus is to articulate succinctly what you're trying to accomplish. Facebook connects people. Google lets you search. Amazon is the place to buy anything online. If you can't make a similarly succinct statement about your mission, you're not focused enough.

You may argue that mission statements are a load of BS for big companies and big organizations. There's some truth to that—the mission statements on those big company web sites—"We strive to decrease the inefficiencies associated with..." are consensus-written hogwash that started out as good ideas but ended up badly.

When it comes to startups, however, a mission statement captures in a sentence or a phrase what it is you're trying to do. It's a rallying cry for your team, whether that team is 1 person or 100. It informs product tradeoffs, marketing messaging, and sales strategy.

Failure to focus comes in many different forms. When people talk about products that are too complex, have too many features, or—trying to be polite—do many things well, what they're really talking about is a lack of focus.

Companies that fail to focus do so because they haven't yet found their market sweet spot, their founders enjoy building product for product's sake, or they're not willing to let go of a product that is no longer core to the business.

Like many startups, after a few years in business, Company Y ended up with two main product lines. On the face of it, this was not a bad thing—the company was generating revenue from both. The products started out as one and then later split into two because a group of customers were interested in a subset of features from the original product.

Over time, the customer bases for the two products became more and more distinct, creating a real challenge for Company Y. The sales strategies and sales people were completely independent, as were the product teams. In reality, the startup was two startups in one.

Company Y's competitors for the second product gradually and then more rapidly began beating Company Y to market. Although Company Y kept winning customers, the competition seemed to be a step ahead on feature set and sales. Engineers became frustrated as they were pulled back and forth between the two product lines. Company Y's management team agonized for months about what to do—they didn't want to "put the wood behind the arrow" of one product or the other; they still believed their original product was the bigger market opportunity, yet they couldn't get themselves to give up the revenue from the second product.

The turning point came in the form of a 1-2-3 punch. The first punch was when a huge deal for Company Y to be acquired fell through because the acquiring company was only interested in the first business, not the second.

Punch number two came during an embarrassing board meeting in which the CEO indicated that both businesses were struggling. The mood in the room was grim.

Then came the third punch: another industry player eagerly wanted the second business, but not the first. The message to Company Y could not have been clearer: the two businesses together were worthless. Separate, they were incredibly valuable. The management team sold off the second business and went on to build a much more valuable company, but not before wasting a year of cash trying to keep both businesses afloat.

The lesson? Quickly take the actions that the market is eventually going to force you to take anyway; don't want for external pressures to force decisions on you. Force them on yourself.

Whether you have too many product lines or too many features, it's easy to deceive yourself into thinking that if your product or your company does many things, at least one of them will appeal to potential users.

The reality is, users don't use a product for its breadth of features. They use it or buy it because it does one thing really well. It solves one huge pain point. When that pain point or unfulfilled need is the same for thousands of customers or millions of users, it creates the potential for a very successful startup.

Too Much Friction to Achieve Adoption

Frequently, companies build products that have the potential to offer tremendous value—if only their users could get started using the products! Consider all the web sites with long sign-up forms, or sites that require users to enter lots of information manually before they can derive value. In contrast, consider a site like Facebook, where a simple address-book import unlocks the majority of the site's value. Once connected to their friends, users can see a steady flow of photos and updates; only later do they need to start making their own posts and uploading their own photos.

For startups selling to businesses, many products require so much setup and customization that potential customers simply aren't willing to make the required up-front investment. Compare Siebel—a sales-management system that required on-premises installation and significant customization—and Salesforce.com, now the dominant sales-management system, which requires no installation and comes preconfigured.

If it takes a long time or a big investment of people or capital to derive value from your product, you need to rethink your product strategy. No amount of marketing and selling can take the place of an easy-to-adopt product that delivers value quickly.

Products That Don't Acquire More Users

In Web 1.0, marketing and sales were almost completely independent of product. Products were built, marketed, and sold—although not necessarily in that order. Some companies pre-marketed their products long before they were available to the public, generating demand. But product was its own thing; sales and marketing were "those people over there." Engineers didn't want to have much to do with marketing and sales, and vice versa. In Web 3.0, product, sales, and marketing go hand in hand.

Today, *product innovation is critical to your acquisition strategy*. The dawn of Web 3.0 has made designing user acquisition into your product from the get-go paramount. This book digs deeper into how sales and marketing relate to product later on.

Companies have long spent the vast majority of their money getting the word out. The Internet opened an incredible new path to the consumer, and although advertising became much more targeted, the value exchange remained the same: spend money to drive brand awareness or to acquire individual customers.

With the advent of the social web, things changed. No longer were marketing, sales, and product separate. Facebook (the product) sold itself—existing users invited new users, creating a new zero-cost user-acquisition model. Gaming company Zynga lets users choose between paying actual money for items and inviting friends in order to obtain those items.

Obviously, not every company can benefit from this kind of pure network effect.[3] But there are many product lessons to be learned from these companies, and this one is the key: today, great products market and sell themselves. A truly great product isn't just one that people want to tell their colleagues and friends about; the product also makes it easy to do so.

Later in the book, I get into some specific tactics for making products of any kind more *viral*—moving through the market in a way that increases the customer base dramatically. But the core point is that your product not only has to be designed from the outset with marketing and sales built in, but it also has

---

[3] With network effects—when they work well—the more users there are of a product, the more valuable the product becomes for those users. Examples include the telephone, Facebook, PayPal, and LinkedIn. Each additional person joining the network makes the network more valuable, and each person derives more value as a result.

to incent existing users to market your product actively to other users because they derive real benefit from doing so.

Simple, Universal, and Viral

Great products are simple, universal, and viral. This applies to consumer products and to business-to-business ones as well:

- *Simple*: The product is easy to use. Its functionality is accessible. It may have lots of features, but they're under the covers, discoverable by users later.

- *Universal:* Whatever you're building is broadly applicable. You can build a good product that only a few people use, but the definition of a great product is one that's adopted by many.

- *Viral:* Your product markets and spreads itself.

Consider Twitter's 140-character limit. Users don't have to think too much about what to do because they're limited to 140 characters. A link is a very easy way to share something you're interested in with others. The product is incredibly easy to use. And users see other users using it, producing a network effect.

Pandora is another great example of sheer simplicity: the Thumbs Up / Thumbs Down buttons as a way to indicate what you like and dislike are brilliantly simple. The rest happens under the covers based on that simple action.

What's an equivalent in a business context? Anti-spam products. Such products of course rely on lots of complex algorithms, models, and data. But they also rely on another very simple action: the Delete key. Delete a message without reading it, and chances are, it's spam.

How can you implement viral marketing in a business product? Granted, it's harder for business products and even more difficult for infrastructure products—products that aren't visible to end users, such as storage and networking gear.

Dropbox is one company crossing the consumer/business divide with its file-storage and -sharing offering. Not only is the product simple to use, but it also gets users to spread the word, both by sharing files and by encouraging users invite their friends to get more storage space. Dropbox also fits a universal rule: everyone needs to store and share files.

What about infrastructure companies? Certainly viral isn't easy to implement when end users aren't involved. But Intel came as close as possible to viral for an infrastructure product—a hardware chip—through its "Intel Inside" campaign. It was by no means zero-cost user acquisition: Intel had to spend millions of dollars on the campaign. But it paid off.

When it comes to infrastructure, the proxy for *viral* is *social pressure*: thus you see ad campaigns like "9 out of 10 *Fortune* 100 companies use X." These are what I call *assisted-viral*. The products themselves are by no means viral, but the companies running these campaigns take advantage of existing customer adoption to drive social pressure and thereby further adoption.

What's more, product reviews are readily accessible online, and business colleagues are connected via networks like LinkedIn. As a result, the word on products—both good and bad—spreads like wildfire. It's easier than ever to get the word out, but it's also harder than ever to escape a bad review.

Whatever your business, make your product incredibly simple to use. The old saying "less is more" could not apply more strongly than to product design.

The Magic of Product Chemistry

The secret sauce of great products is *product chemistry*. Product chemistry is when all the ingredients of a product—all the features—work well together. It takes a lot of trial and error to get there. This seems obvious, yet it's often overlooked. Far too many products consist of interesting features that fail to deliver a "sum is greater than the parts" experience.

When you have chemistry, you know it. You feel it—in your product, in your team, and in the entire execution of your company. If one company epitomizes product chemistry today, it's Apple.

In contrast, the Apple Newton, an early personal digital assistant, was an example of a product that didn't quite have chemistry. Although Apple invested some $100 million in Newton development, the product never took off due to delays, feature creep, and other issues. It was a visionary product that presaged what became today's iPhone and Android devices, but it failed because it lacked product chemistry.

If you're two or three years into the business, growing, but not where you want to be, it may be because you're missing product chemistry. Perhaps you've built out a lot of features to meet the demands of users or customers, or you've wandered around in search of product-market fit. Regardless, to gain widespread adoption, you have to create the kind of chemistry that early adopters were willing to live without.

Just because you're a product and market visionary with an incredible nose for finding product-market fit doesn't mean you're a great product designer. Great product design is about all the pieces fitting together, about style, about ease of use: bringing the core to the forefront while making more advanced features accessible but not intrusive. Product chemistry requires all the features not just to be designed well individually, but to be designed to work well together.

How do you know a great design? It just feels right. A great design is like a work of art; you can break it down into its parts and analyze what makes it great, but it can't be reconstructed simply by putting all those components together. Great designs come from great designers.

If you're a few years into your company, and you're seeing adoption of your product, but it's slow going, stop and ask yourself if your design is truly great enough to gain widespread adoption. If it's not, hire a designer—and keep in mind that great design doesn't come through consensus. People frequently comment about the elegance and simplicity of Apple products. That is a core part of the product focus and key to the greatness of the experience.

What's more, in today's market, product chemistry is expected. Apple has set the bar for well-designed products; and consumers, even when they're in business situations, expect great design. They expect products to look and feel good and all the features to work well together. When it comes to gaining widespread adoption, don't underestimate the importance of ease of use, great design, and the pieces all working well together.

Don't Ship Too Early or Too Late

There are two schools of thought on product delivery. One is "Ship early, ship often." The other is, "Don't ship until it's ready." Both are right. Like so many things in startups, the challenge is finding the balance that works for you.

On the one hand, if you release a product to market too early—if it's buggy or lacks critical features—potential users won't use it. But if you wait too long, you may discover no one wants to use your product or that a competitor has emerged and taken the market lead, and you've consumed all your capital in the process.

This is why you must have at least *one user* for your product. Sounds simple: one user! That user can be either you or someone else. If you're building for yourself, of course, the process is a lot easier. You know what you want. The question is whether anyone else wants the same thing. But if no one is using your product—if it stays in the back room too long—you risk ending up with a lot of technology that no one really wants.

It hardly seems possible, but Startup A suffered from shipping both too early and too late. Startup A's founder built the company's initial product over a weekend. It was the classic Silicon Valley story. The product solved a personal problem for him. It turned out much later that millions of people had that same problem and were willing to spend money to solve it.

Unfortunately for the founder of Startup A, he wasn't the one to benefit. That's because his company never built a product that many other people could use. Startup A's product had so many rough edges that although users were willing to try it—based on the promise that it would solve their problems—they weren't willing to stick with it. Using the product was too difficult. By the time the founder of Startup A admitted this was an issue, the market had passed him by—he was too late. One of Startup A's competitors grew to more than $100 million in revenue and recently filed to go public.

Startup B built software that worked with some of the largest hardware manu-facturers on the planet. Unfortunately, Startup B was in such a rush to get its product out that when it landed its first big customer, the customer discov-ered tons of bugs in the product. To be fair to Startup B, the hardware partner didn't commit sufficient resources to integrating the hardware and software—but the blame fell on Startup B regardless. How could Startup B have avoided the problem? By working a lot more closely with its big-brother partner to begin with.

Then there is the story of Startup C, which started out doing one thing, put it out there early, and realized very few people would use the product. The founders rapidly reframed the same basic product offering but with a different message and market. The result was tens of millions of very happy users. Had the founders waited, they might have missed the market completely.

If there is one company that represents perfection in products, it's Apple. In reality, however, Apple has had years to test what works—and what doesn't—from the original Mac to the Apple Newton.

When it comes to startups, it's better to ship earlier than later. Once you've gotten market feedback, however, you must be willing to invest the time to take what is most likely an 80% offering (at best) and redesign it until it "just works." Fail to tackle the remaining 20%, and the market will pass you by and adopt other products.

Products That Don't Scale

Some products that appear ready for production are, in reality, prototypes. They were never built to support large numbers of users, the source code is hard to maintain, and they contain inherent design flaws that make them slow at scale. Yet designing and implementing for scale takes time and costs money. How do you avoid over-designing your product so that you can release it quickly and get real-world feedback, while still making sure the product can support millions of users if you attain the success to which you aspire?

Accept that your product will be rewritten at least once. I used to believe products could be and should be built properly from the ground up. But nearly every early-stage entrepreneur tries multiple product concepts before finding the one that works. If these entrepreneurs had over-invested in scale from the beginning, they would have run out of money before they had a chance to test the market for their product.

The challenge is that when a product takes off, it's extremely hard to put the brakes on mid-scale. Friendster, one of the pioneers of the social-networking space, lost its market lead in large part because it failed to scale. Performance issues caused pages on the site to take so long to load that users abandoned the site. The company had clearly found a market need, yet it focused on adding new features rather than revisiting its foundation and architecture. The company also faced a challenge similar to that faced by other pioneers; not only did it have to find product-market fit and build its product, but it also had to build core infrastructure to support its product.

The answer to product scaling, then, is to design first for the fast discovery of product-market fit and then be not only willing but adamant about focusing on the design and architecture required to scale. The good news at least for web-based startups is that much of the infrastructure and expertise required to scale are available. The decision to stop adding features and invest in scale, of course, is one only you can make.

Summary

Great products are at the heart of today's leading startups. No longer is product independent of sales and marketing. And well-designed consumer-technology products have raised the overall expectation of product simplicity, both at home and at work.

Bad products get built due to lack of

- Product vision

- Focus

- Users

These problems are solved through

- A succinctly articulated goal

- A great product that is broadly applicable

- Using your own product (or finding a close equivalent)

CHAPTER 3

The Missing Entrepreneur

Market Visionary and Product Picker

Missing entrepreneur? I know what you're thinking: "Every startup has an entrepreneur." What I mean is an entrepreneur with a capital E. Let me explain: a lot of people have good ideas, and some are even able to execute on them. But rare is the man or woman who can take an idea and transform it into a sharply defined product and then sell it to top-level prospective hires, investors, and customers. An Entrepreneur, as opposed to their lowercase counterpart, is a product picker and a market visionary. A great Entrepreneur seeks out a great market. A little e entrepreneur, lacking strong product and market vision, burns through cash as the team struggles to define its position.

An Entrepreneur with a Capital *E*

A colleague once told me that making successful investments is much like going to the horse races. To win, you've got to pick the right race, the right horse, and the right jockey. I've never been to the horse races, only the startup races, but I still love this analogy when it comes to thinking about how to build a successful company.

I've talked at length about the race and the horse. And later in the book, I get into the gory details of teams and how to overcome the challenges of execution and scaling. But in this chapter I want to focus on *the Entrepreneur with a capital E* because without this individual, startups simply wouldn't exist.

An Entrepreneur with a capital E is a market visionary and unparalleled product picker. The best Entrepreneurs seek out large markets—to create or disrupt them—and then iterate the product to find product-market fit while not running out of cash. Sometimes they find it out of the gate; other times it takes years.

Entrepreneurs with a capital E often have very wide apertures as they cycle through new idea after new idea; but once they latch onto the right idea, they become ultra-focused. Some entrepreneurs get stuck in iteration mode, jumping from one feature to the next or one idea to the next. Others latch onto an idea too soon, and get stuck at a *local maximum*—a small market they can never execute their way out of.

Entrepreneurs with a capital E tend to have at least a few other characteristics in common. Many are natural promoters. They've had to hustle and sell all their lives, they crave attention, or they have a desire to see the world operate according to their vision of it. Others may not start out as promoters—many entrepreneurs are actually introverts—but ultimately become promoters either out of necessary or because they're forced into being the visible face of their successful companies. Michael Dell is one famous example.

Finally, Entrepreneurs with a capital E have incredible self-determination. They have a need to challenge themselves and grow, and they're frequently unwilling to settle. They're hungry: hungry to prove they're right, hungry for success, and hungry to disrupt and transform big markets. They don't stop at being visionaries—they execute on their vision by signing up other people to turn their vision into reality.

Where's Marc?

Marc Benioff, Bill Gates, Steve Jobs, Larry Ellison, Larry and Sergey, Mark Zuckerberg, and Jeff Bezos, to name a few, are all clearly Entrepreneurs with a capital E. They were instrumental to the creation and success of their companies.

Without Benioff, for example, Salesforce.com wouldn't have become the category-defining company that it did. So when an entrepreneur starts an investment pitch with a statement like, "We're like Salesforce.com except for..." the number-one question in the audience's mind isn't "How similar is this company to Salesforce.com?" Rather, it's "Is this entrepreneur the next Marc Benioff?"

Some might minimize the impact of this missing factor on the potential success of their business. But if you look at the most successful tech companies of the last 20 or 30 years, there are almost always one or two key people you can point to who made the company. Conversely, few people remember who was at the head of the failures. Don't just ask yourself what it takes to pitch like an Entrepreneur with a capital E. Ask yourself what it takes to *be* one.

An Entrepreneur's Quest: The Big Idea

If one thing separates big E Entrepreneurs from little e entrepreneurs, it's *The Big Idea*. *The Big Idea* describes the way the Entrepreneur's company will transform The Big Market. The Big Idea isn't about the details, the features, or the practicalities of today. It's about how the world will be tomorrow, after the Entrepreneur's vision/dream becomes reality.

Some Entrepreneurs set out with The Big Idea, but not all do. Sometimes, entrepreneurs start building product and only later realize they have a vision for something big—something game-changing. That is the moment when they go from being entrepreneurs to being Entrepreneurs. They have The Big Idea, they articulate it, and they do everything in their power to make it a reality.

The Big Idea is what potential employees and investors fall in love with. It's what motivates them to invest their time and money. It's what keeps them going even when the day-to-day is a brutal challenge. The product is the implementation of The Big Idea. When people use the product, that is the realization of the Entrepreneur's dream: the Entrepreneur's vision has become reality.

Picking the Right Product for Your Market

Big E founders have an excellent sense of the market they intend to dominate. There are many different ways to find your market. Some entrepreneurs have an experience with one way of solving a problem and decide that problem should be solved in a different way. Marc Benioff started Salesforce.com for that very reason.

Often, entrepreneurs start with a big market and then stumble around in search of the right opportunity. In reality, that stumbling around is a fundamental part of finding product-market fit.

I remember when my co-founders and I were starting our first company. Our excitement about starting something new was surpassed only by our naiveté. We spent a few months—which at the time seemed like an eternity on the few hundred thousand dollars in capital we had raised—doing what seemed like floundering around.

Finally, we built a system for sending text messages over wireless networks. We went out and talked to customers to see if they'd buy it. Sometimes our text messages went through, other times they didn't. We were we having a hard time getting customers to buy our product, but we were having an even harder time getting the messages to go through reliably! When we tried to do a demo with a customer and our messages wouldn't go through, naturally they assumed our product didn't work.

To address the issue, we built a service to measure whether messages were being sent and received properly. Customers weren't buying our real product, but one day we happened to mention our measurement system. "We have that exact problem!" the vice president we were talking to exclaimed in front of his team. We had never heard that before, and when we got back to the office we agonized over what to do. We didn't have enough resources or capital to deliver both systems simultaneously. We had to pick one or the other. We went with the measurement service.

I used to wish I could say we had the foresight to build the measurement service from the beginning. The reality was that we chose an interesting and rapidly growing market. We made an initial assertion about what product to build. It wasn't what the market wanted, but it was adjacent to what the market wanted.

As a result, we were there to capture the opportunity when it arose. The insight was to take what seemed like our side product and make it what the business was all about. What felt at the time like floundering around was in reality the natural process of finding our product-market fit.

Teams Without a Clear Vision Fail

Small e founders often lead teams that execute without a clear vision. As the old saying goes, if you don't know where you're going, any road will get you there. You may wonder how this can possibly happen.

There's the romantic notion of starting something—be your own boss, run your own show, and build what you want to build. The reality can be somewhat different. A team can start out with a clear vision. But after discovering that people either don't want to use what they've built or want to use it but don't want to pay for it, the team loses its way. Team members get stuck in a sort of no-man's land with an existing product and some users, but no bigger picture vision of how they want to transform the market and what they need to build to do so. Some founders aren't sure what their target market is. They're stuck being small e entrepreneurs.

This was the situation of Company T, a composite, whose founder built a product and raised venture capital. A great technologist, but not a market visionary, the founder built a product that was difficult to use. He did little to promote a larger vision of how it would transform the market. The company added customers, but its revenues stayed more or less flat. Investors described the company as having gone sideways—it didn't go out of business, but it wasn't growing.

At the same time, the founder of Company T didn't have a clear vision for himself—he vacillated between wanting to raise a lot of capital to grow and staying small so that he could remain in his comfort zone. Meanwhile, his fixed costs (the costs of paying for employees, rent, hosting costs, and the like) stayed the same, chewing through the small amount of capital he had raised.

Several years later, two new companies started in the same space. Their founders articulated clear visions of how they were transforming the space and the key trends they were riding to do so. On that basis and the simplicity of their products, they were able to raise tens of millions of dollars in venture capital.

All three companies went after the same market. The difference? The founders of the two successful companies had very clear visions for themselves and their markets. They built highly focused and elegantly simple products as a result. That enabled them to accomplish their goals and fulfill their aspirations.

Money Doesn't Help When You Don't Have Users

Big *E* Entrepreneurs are all about finding product-market fit. That means they're experts at building something people want and driving user adoption.

Simply put, there are two ways to make sure you have enough runway to find product-market fit. You can raise lots of money or spend frugally. Even if you can raise a lot of money, I recommend against it until you have product-market fit. Companies have a tendency to spend the money they raise. Lots of capital is critical for scaling when you're ready to grow. But if you're still searching for product-market fit, too much capital makes it easy to lose focus. It's all too easy to hire more resources rather than make hard tradeoffs. In the worst case, it can cause a company's founders to get comfortable, reducing their sense of urgency. It also makes it too simple to build up a large organization that's difficult to change when you figure out you don't have product-market fit.

Entrepreneur S was an incredibly talented software engineer who worked at a large Silicon Valley software company. Based on the strength of his reputation and where he worked, when he left to start his own company, multiple investors offered him large amounts of money on great terms. In under a month, he and his team raised $10 million: $5 million each from two venture firms. Entrepreneur S had joined his previous employer early enough to make millions of dollars, and he walked and talked with the swagger of success.

Some investors assumed that Entrepreneur S had played a large part in the success of the rocket ship that was his previous employer. Others believed he had learned enough from working at his previous employer to be able to apply what he had learned at his new company.

However, Entrepreneur S's previous employer was already a rocket ship by the time he joined. It had exponential growth, users were flocking to it, and it quickly became the dominant market leader.

Although Entrepreneur S led a lot of product innovation, he had not had to suffer through the initial stages of product-market iteration, helping the company find its first users, its first hundred thousand users, and then its first million. He assumed that if he built a great product, users would buy it, because that's what he was fortunate enough to experience in his career; he knew of no other kind of market.

It turned out that Entrepreneur S told a compelling story and had great product ideas, but he was neither a market visionary nor a better-than-average product picker. He was surprised when users didn't show up, taken aback that he had to spend money on marketing, and ultimately—as he was forced to pivot from his original business model—aghast that he had to hire salespeople.

His investors brought in a CEO to run the company. In a rare turn of events, the CEO turned out to be very much an entrepreneur himself. Building off the same product, he moved the company up-market to where he smelled money, went out and got specific customer feedback on requirements, and, combined with some good timing and luck, was able to turn the company into a success.

For Entrepreneur S, the result was bittersweet. The company burned through two rounds of funding while it was figuring out product-market fit, and his equity was significantly diluted in the process.

Dave Duffield, founder of PeopleSoft (acquired by Oracle) and now founder and co-CEO of Workday, is one of the most inspiring big *E* customer advocates around. He's so focused on customers that he not only goes out of his way to use his customer's products but also buys their stock. His mantra is that those companies will be more successful as a result of using his products—so he invests in them! In one example, he doesn't buy shoes just anywhere: he buys them from Zappos, a Workday customer. Of course, this approach makes for great marketing and sales, too; his customers love hearing how he's using their products and buying their stock.

Hire for Operations

Startup success comes down to right market, team, product, timing, and execution. Little e entrepreneurs miss one or more of these fundamental elements.

Whether they realize it or not, the vast majority of people who work at successful technology companies, unless they started them or joined very early, expect customer demand and business models to be in place already. Their jobs are primarily about execution for growth. They introduce product features, implement marketing strategies, and sell to drive broader adoption around the existing core business, while scaling the business infrastructure to support that adoption. The ability to scale is critical to building a large, successful company.

This is not, however, the primary job of an Entrepreneur with a capital *E*—not initially, anyway. Being able to hire people who have the experience to scale is what separates those entrepreneurs who are able to scale with their companies from those who aren't. But hiring those people before you're ready for them limits your options and creates frustration for both you and them.

Frequently, when investors fire entrepreneurs from their own companies, they cite the founder's "inability to scale" as the reason. Sometimes this means the company hasn't found product-market fit and the investors mistakenly hope that bringing in a professional manager will solve the problem. This rarely works because when it comes to startups, professional managers are best at helping startups scale, not doing market discovery. These companies often end up improving marketing, sales, and operations, all while burning through hard-earned capital, only to discover they still don't have a product that a large market wants.

Other times, it means the company is unable to raise money, and the existing investors hope that potential new investors will back the new CEO—often on the basis of their reputation. But most often an "inability to scale" means an entrepreneur is unwilling or unable to hire the management team needed to scale the company.

The unwilling entrepreneur keeps finding reasons to turn down potentially great hires. Whether they admit it or not, these little e entrepreneurs often feel threatened by those with significantly more experience. And conversely, those with more experience tend not to want to work for these little e entrepreneurs. For other entrepreneurs, it's a matter of control—they have trouble delegating responsibility to others, fearing that the job won't be done the way they want.

Then there are those who are propped up by board members just enough so they can get by without the key hires they should be making. This strategy works for a while, but ultimately these companies can't keep up with the efficiency and speed of their competition, which has the best people working on scaling full time.

The best entrepreneurs attract great people, and they make it their mission in life to bring great people into their companies. When they meet a great person, their first question isn't "What open role do I have that this person could fill?" Rather, it's "How do I get this world-class individual involved in my company?" They take great pride in attracting the most talented people and convincing those people to come work at their companies. That is, they see highly qualified, experienced individuals as assets, not threats.

How to Hire Great People

Entrepreneurs often ask me how they can recognize a great executive if they've never before hired a VP of sales or marketing, among other roles. I remember one entrepreneur who told me it was very easy to hire engineers: simply give them a tough problem and see how they solve it!

But hiring executives for other roles seems much more subjective. A lot of times, people who look great on paper aren't so great in reality. This is often the case with executives coming from big companies who turn out not to be able to adapt to the realities of startups, as well as executives who have spent their entire careers in very small companies and don't know how to scale any more than the founder does.

This is where board members and advisors—but perhaps most critically, simulations—are invaluable. One of the best executives I have ever worked with, having narrowed the potential hires down to two, brings them both in for full afternoon sessions with the team. This isn't a one-on-one interview—that has already happened. Rather, it's a real live discussion as if the potential hire already had the job. For a VP of sales, that means a full pipeline review; for a head of marketing, working through an actual marketing plan. Is this approach time consuming? Absolutely. But it's far less time consuming than making the wrong hire.

By going through this simulation with both hires, the hiring executive and the rest of the team also have a live point of comparison; they're not trying to make a decision in the absence of any reference point or in comparison to a potential hire they saw weeks before and who they therefore may be remembering incorrectly. The cost to you and the organization of churning through a mis-hire is very high; so too is the cost to the person who is hired and then let go. Experienced executives know this, and many have experienced that organizational cost themselves. As a result, the very best executives are no more eager to land in the wrong job and have to restart than you are to hire the wrong executive for the job.

One of the biggest struggles I have experienced personally and have seen other founders go through is the challenge of hiring people outside their founding team when the founding team itself is unable to scale: a new head of sales, a more experienced VP of marketing, and so on. Entrepreneurs by nature tend to be incredibly loyal, and the challenge is finding a balance between that loyalty to the original team and bringing in executives who can help scale the organization.

Before a company is scaling, the answer to most questions is, "Figure it out. Try something else and see if it works." But when your company is starting to scale, the answer to the question "How do I do X?" is almost always "Hire someone who knows how to do that." Do what you're good at—hire for what you're not. Again, this is how Entrepreneurs operate.

Always Act Like an Entrepreneur

At some point or another, some Entrepreneurs stop acting like Entrepreneurs. They stop taking the big risks because they have invested so much in the current path that they become concerned about deviating from it. I remember a call from an entrepreneur who wanted my advice. He had been able to raise a lot of capital on the strength of his vision and his team. He was generating a lot of buzz, receiving a ton of PR coverage, and getting meetings with potential customers and partners at the very highest levels. What he was doing had the potential to be incredibly strategic.

He confided in me that he had a terrible feeling that his current strategy wasn't going to work. This was more than just a moment of self doubt. Founders have a way of knowing when something fundamental is wrong—from a bug causing a slowdown in their web site to their overall strategy—even if they can't articulate exactly what it is. He had that feeling.

During the phone call, he asked me questions he never would have asked when he was starting out. "What will people think if I totally change the strategy? What will my board think?" And, of course, there was the question he left unasked—would his investors fire him because he had raised money on one strategy and now wanted to implement a different one?

I asked him why he was hesitating, when he already knew the decision he had to make. By this point, the company had more than 50 employees, and he had just hired a senior sales executive who had relocated to close the deals he hadn't been able to close himself.

"I'd have to tell the board we were changing the strategy, fire the sales exec I just hired, and lay off 20 people. And I'm worried about the competition." Silence hung in the air. I had never heard so much fear and worry in this entrepreneur's voice before. His psyche was eating him up. It was no time to mince words. "It's either that or lay off the whole company after you burn through your cash," I replied. He called a special board meeting and took action.

Focus on What You're Great At

Should you spend time improving your weaknesses or focus on what you're great at? Although it may be deceptively appealing to try to improve the areas you and your company are weak at, in competitive markets, startups win on being better and being differentiated. You can't differentiate by improving your weaknesses, either as a company or as a person. As an entrepreneur, your company lives or dies based on whether it can be great at one thing—not whether it can be good at many. Plus, you can hire to backfill your weaknesses.

Consider Google: great at search. Facebook: great at connecting people. Before these companies were great at many things, they were great at one thing. They did that one thing better than any other company in the world. Later, they added lots of features and improved in related areas. But they first became the best at one thing.

Investors often argue that a startup that is great at just one thing is a feature, not a product or a company. The reality is, many of the most successful companies are features, but features that address market needs so vast that huge, valuable companies are built around them to support that one feature.

Starting vs. Leading

Because you have to hold so many jobs when your company is starting out, it's easy to believe that you have to improve your weaknesses to become a great leader. The reality is, after you're done starting and once you find product-market fit, you just have to be great at leading.

That's easier said than done, of course. Starting is about failing at lots of different approaches quickly, until you find the right one. Leading is about taking what's succeeding and growing it. Not all company starters enjoy leading.

Starting gives an Entrepreneur a clean slate. Although the vast majority of people may find a clean slate terrifying, for the Entrepreneur, a clean slate is the great liberator. There are no legacy users to support or old features to maintain. There is no organizational history, layers of management, extreme compensation differences, or political jockeying for position.

Leading requires getting people to set all those differences aside to work together as a team. Leaders can't just build—they have to be available to those they're leading.

Entrepreneur E was an extrovert in the most extreme sense of the word. He thrived on being out with users and customers, talking to people, and selling. It didn't matter whether he was selling to potential customers, hiring employees, speaking at conferences, or pitching investors. He loved being out there—and he thrived on and needed the attention that came with constant pitching and selling.

Entrepreneur I was an introvert. A talented engineer, he had been head of engineering at a large company where he had risen through the ranks to manage a large team. But he never had to set company direction; whenever questions came up about product or company direction, he leaned on the direction the CEO had laid out.

Both Entrepreneurs E and I were terrible leaders. Both told their people that they were always available and people should feel free to talk with them directly at any time. But Entrepreneur E was so outwardly focused that he spent little time in the office. He lacked empathy, and his own people were afraid to work with him or bring up issues for fear that they would bruise his ego and he would fire them. Conversely, Entrepreneur I would sit in his office with his headphones on, working on the product. In their own way, each lacked engagement with their companies once they started to scale, and they failed to be leaders as a result.

Going from a starting role to a leadership role is one of the toughest transitions any entrepreneur has to make. What if you're not a great leader? Either put your mind to becoming one, or hire someone who is.

Fail Fast

Entrepreneurship involves repeated failure, and sometimes very public failure. Your response to this failure determines your survival as an entrepreneur.

To be an entrepreneur, you must internally believe that you're right, even in the face of many smart people telling you that you're wrong. By implication, then, entrepreneurs must have large egos; whether they expose those egos to others in the form of arrogance is, of course, a separate question. For some entrepreneurs, because so much confidence is required to keep believing they're right, confidence in one area is often accompanied by immense insecurity in many others.

The challenge of being an Entrepreneur with a capital *E* ultimately comes down to managing your own ego or finding a belief system that supports it. Rather than seeing more experienced hires as threats, for example, those hires are ego builders. Bad at lots of things? No problem. Startup success is about being great at one thing. In large part, then, the art of being an Entrepreneur with a capital *E* is figuring out how to manage your ego not through the highs of success but through the lows of failure.

Failing fast is healthier for your ego, and it's also healthier for your company and your wallet. I recall one company that spent more than $100 million and 6 years before admitting its product was a failure. You may wonder why the company's investors continued to fund it all that time. The simple truth: They didn't want to admit failure either.

To be an entrepreneur requires stubbornness and persistence. Sometimes, however, this persistence can lead entrepreneurs to try to make a bad product or a bad market work for far longer than they should. The faster you figure out what the market doesn't want, the sooner you can figure out what it does want. That, of course, leads to success.

Summary

An Entrepreneur with a capital *E* is at the heart of any new company. As the old saying goes, if you don't know where you're going, any road will get you there. Startups that have great execution but lack a clear vision can make short-term progress but can never obtain long-term success.

Be an Entrepreneur with a capital *E*:

- Be a market visionary.

- Disrupt and transform a big, existing market, or create a new one.

- Relentlessly pursue product-market fit.

- Deliver a product that addresses the market need.

- Promote your vision to support your business.

- Use failure to get to success.

- Start—and then lead.

Sales and Marketing

It's easy to take hard-won capital and spend it aggressively on sales and marketing. But it's impossible to get that money back if you invest it in the wrong product or the wrong go-to-market approach.

But how do you know whether you're ready to pour gas on the fire? In Chapter 4, I'll discuss how to know whether you really have product-market fit, and what to do if you don't. I'll introduce two key tools: the Sales Learning Curve and Net Promoter Score, and I'll describe how you can put them to work quickly and easily. And I'll talk about the impact traction has on how investors value your company—and what you can do to influence that valuation.

It's not enough to build a great product—you also have to sell it efficiently. Ultimately, building a successful company comes down to acquiring users or customers efficiently. In Chapter 5, we'll add another tool to the toolbox, Customer Lifetime Value, which will answer the key question: how much can you afford to spend to acquire a customer? I'll cover a number of avoidable yet common sales mistakes—from ineffective sales people to bad contracts. And we'll get into some exciting new sales approaches, such as the freemium model, that you can use to get your sales engine humming.

Of course, if no one's ever heard of your company other than a handful of friends, you're not going to have much success in the market. But today, marketing doesn't have to be costly. In Chapter 6 you'll learn the seven proven ways to market your startup and your products.

Part II will give you the tools you need to avoid sales and marketing failure—and to sell and market efficiently and effectively.

Investing in Sales and Marketing Too Early

Know When to Spend—and When Not To

Many companies move to a high burn rate too quickly, and it's hard to go back. Sometimes even frugal entrepreneurs wind up spending too much either because they don't manage the money or are tempted by having money in the bank. This often happens when a startup raises too much money too early. It also happens with entrepreneurs who are accustomed to having lots of resources—for example, if they've spent time at big companies. Frequently it happens when entrepreneurs haven't found product-market fit and believe that it's just a matter of spending money to reach the right customers or users.

The Real Cost of Spending Too Early

For every venture dollar invested, I estimate that more than two-thirds goes into sales and marketing costs and only a third into product development. Spending on sales and marketing too early means there is no return if customers don't bite. These dollars, unlike those invested in product, can't be leveraged if a company is trying to sell product consumers, or customers simply don't want to buy. Once you up the burn rate, there's no easy way back.

Many startups ramp up sales before the product is ready. Of course, a lot of work is required to get sales early on. But a product with a truly great value proposition that delivers in a measurable way practically sells itself.

The right time to invest heavily in sales and marketing is when you've determined that you have product-market fit. When you've reached that inflection point, then—and only then—should you spend aggressively on sales and marketing to drive growth. Companies that ramp sales and marketing too soon waste a lot of money. That problem compounds itself, leading to wasted financing rounds, dilution of equity, and, often, loss of your own job.

Sometimes, even when you have a great product, you don't understand the sales process well enough to scale it. You need to know who you're selling to, how much they will really spend, and what kind of salesperson the company needs to hire who can succeed at selling that particular product to those people. All of this must be understood before sales can efficiently scale.

Of course, some startups don't need to spend heavily on sales and marketing—their products are designed to market themselves. The next two chapters get into that in more detail.

CEO X, an incredible promoter, naturally got investors excited about his company. In two years, he raised three rounds of funding with just a few million dollars in annual revenue—most of which came at a loss. That is, he was spending so heavily on acquiring new customers that the company was far from profitable. Both he and his investors interpreted the revenue as an indicator of having found product-market fit and concluded that if they spent more on marketing, they could drive a lot more revenue.

No one wanted to believe, given the amount of capital raised and the associated valuation, that the company was still pre-product-market fit. Moreover, CEO X's investors weren't on the same page. The early investors helped convince the later ones that the company was ready for a growth round; the later investors—having invested on the belief that the company was ready to grow quickly and having promised that to their partners and their own investors—didn't want to admit that the company wasn't ready to scale. This is another reason not to raise too much capital too early: not only does doing so create a lack of alignment, but it's also very hard to live up to the expectations that come with that capital and the associated valuation.

When the company failed to achieve its projected sales two quarters in a row, the board gave CEO X feedback that he should replace the head of sales. He did. The new head of sales turned over the entire sales team but told the board it would take as much as two full quarters for each new sales representative to become fully productive.

With the burn still incredibly high and sales limping along, the board and management team finally concluded that the company hadn't found product-market fit. Total time consumed (or, more accurately, wasted): four quarters.

The real measure of whether a startup is ready to invest in growth is if it's clear that the company can acquire users or customers in a repeatable and efficient manner. Ultimately, of course, that acquisition has to be both efficient and profitable.

Ratcheting Up the Burn Is Easy—Bringing It Down Is Difficult

It's easy to spend money on marketing quickly. Open a Google AdWords account, put in your credit card, and set the budget to a few thousand dollars per day. Combine that with hiring like there's no tomorrow, and you're off to the races. If the condition of the United States economy is any indicator, it's easy to spend money—but not so easy to save it.

In an ideal world, companies would be able to scale their organizations up and down just as they do their computing resources. The difference is, there is a hidden cost to scaling down organizations. The negative impact on the organization is expensive.

As anyone who has managed an organization can attest, organizations don't operate one person at a time. There are teams and groups. It may be easy for investors to tell a company to "cut the burn," but the human beings that make up organizations are slow to recover from these sorts of cost-cutting exercises.

The cost also affects founders/employees disproportionately as compared to investors. Professional investors can keep writing checks to buy more equity, but founders and employees can't create more equity. Thus, burning through capital unnecessarily tends to hurt founders and employees more than it hurts investors.

But if you've scaled your company prematurely, you must cut the burn. These cuts take a long time to heal. We've all heard stories of companies making repeated cuts. Company leadership is trying to "do the right thing" by keeping people in their jobs, yet employees live in fear that they may be the next to go. Better to cut too deep than too shallow.

Investors may seem schizophrenic, sometimes encouraging you to cut the burn while at other times suggesting you spend aggressively. This is because investors have very few levers once they have invested. They can push you to spend less, they can invest more, or they can fire you and hire someone else.

Of course, investors perform many other activities: making introductions to customers, potential employees, and other investors. They can also help you make strategic decisions and, of course, ensure a company's ultimate liquidity. But when it comes to day-to-day operations, there is very little they can do. At the same time, they may feel intense pressure to do something when a company appears not to be working.

When a company hits its growth inflection point, it should raise as much capital as it can and grow as quickly and aggressively as possible. Scaling prematurely, however, is incredibly costly—not just in terms of capital but in terms of organizational health as well.

Don't Mistake a Lack of Product-Market Fit for Poor Execution

All too often, people confuse a lack of product-market fit with a failure to execute. Experienced operating executives often believe that if they can get the right team in place—in particular, the right lead-generation and sales operations—they can solve what appears to be an execution issue.

They get things running smoothly, only to discover that the product still isn't selling. Perhaps customers seem interested, but they just aren't buying.

Common refrains include, "We need a different go-to-market strategy," "We'll get a new VP of sales with a team who can actually sell," and "We haven't been trying this approach long enough to know if it works." Or, in the case of consumer startups, "We just need to get this in front of more users."

Management and board members alike simply don't want to believe—especially after ratcheting up the burn rate—that the product doesn't meet a market need. Or, if it does meet a market need, they don't want to accept that it has too much friction to gain adoption—it's too difficult for people to use or buy.

How can you tell which problem you have? Find out how happy your existing customers are. If they're happy, and a lot of other potential customers could derive the same value, then you have a go-to-market/execution problem. If they're happy, but it's because of something unique to their business, you have a product-market fit problem. If they're unhappy, you have a product problem.

Granted, it's not a question of product-market fit *or* execution. Great startups get both right. What's critical is not to confuse a lack of one for a lack of the other.

Understand the Traction Curve

How do you know when you're ready to invest aggressively in sales and marketing? Mark Leslie, former CEO of storage-management company Veritas Software and now a lecturer at the Stanford Graduate School of Business, first introduced me to the Sales Learning Curve (SLC) when I took his sales operations course at Stanford. Although it's primarily business (not consumer) focused, it's one of the best tools available for figuring out when you're ready to invest in scale.

In the past, one of the biggest questions startup founders faced was whether they could build the product. That is still an open question outside of information technology. For example, biotechnology companies face fundamental science risks, and clean-tech companies face questions about whether they can convert from prototype scale to production scale. But for the vast majority of business and consumer software companies, the question isn't whether they can build the product but whether people will use it once it's built—and whether the companies can develop an efficient approach for reaching their potential customers.

Many companies can now rely on open source software and cloud-based infrastructure like Amazon Web Services to provide the basic building blocks for their products. Even today's hardware companies are in large part software. As a result, startups can and must spend more of their time and capital engineering efficient customer adoption into their products and honing their go-to-market strategies.

Leslie describes three distinct phases of the SLC:

- *Initiation phase:* A startup is trying to get customers. The company is still very much in a period of discovery and learning, refining both its product and its approach to selling that product.

- *Transition phase:* Sales are beginning to accelerate. The company has real market traction.

- *Execution phase:* The company is ready to invest aggressively.

One key insight from the SLC is that the slope of the customer-adoption curve steepens rapidly as companies move through the transition phase. Thus, before you start spending aggressively on marketing and hiring lots of sales people, ask yourself whether your adoption curve is really steepening. If it's not, you're still in the initiation phase.

Company X hired an extremely experienced VP of sales who then hired a complete team of sales reps to sell the company's product. But the company—which had very complex technology at its core—hadn't yet figured out how to package its offering so that customers could see a clear value proposition that was easy to buy into.

Although customers expressed a lot of interest in solving the pain point that Company X's product addressed, few actually purchased the product. All the while, the company kept burning through cash and missing its numbers. It was another year before the company figured out how to package its product in such a way that it was easy for customers to buy. In reality, the company was still in the initiation phase. It shouldn't have ramped up sales until it figured this it out.

Where business startups must prove a repeatable sales model, consumer startups must prove a repeatable user-acquisition model—and they must continue to maintain their growth. Yet the principles of the SLD still apply: the slope of the *net* adoption curve—the number of new users minus those who leave—must steepen aggressively to justify spending aggressively on sales and marketing.

I emphasize *net* adoption curve because many consumer startups have been known to spend aggressively on acquisition in support of growth only to have a large percentage of their users churn out and the curve eventually flatten. It doesn't help to acquire a lot of users if your product isn't sticky enough to get them to continue using it.

Create Unique Value

There are examples of creating value without following the SLC, of course. Some companies spend aggressively on sales and marketing before they have figured out how to make those sales profitable—and their founders and investors make lots of money in the process.

But these companies require very unique market and capital environments to support their growth. Daily deal site Groupon is one example. The company has seen incredible sales growth, going from $30 million in 2009 to $313 million in 2010 to $430.2 million for the third quarter of 2011. Yet during that same record third quarter, the company accrued expenses and payables of $622 million to merchants.

The company's recent IPO valued it at more than $17 billion. Whether the company's model is sustainable is an open question. But the founders made a lot of money in the process, and so did investors. The founders took hundreds of millions of dollars off the table as part of a previous (private) round of funding. And on paper, at least, the ownership positions of both the founders and investors are now worth billions. Clearly, value was created—but again, it required a very unique market and capital environment.

A key question to ask yourself is what kind of company you want to build. Many companies lose money for years; some are even unprofitable after they go public. Although investors may claim to want to build stand-alone companies that will be around for a long, long time, the primary goal of most is to make large amounts of money for themselves and their investors.

Founders often put a lot of emphasis on reaching break-even. I commend this goal. It's an absolute necessity in tight capital markets or if you don't want to rely on outside capital. But reaching break-even by itself doesn't make for a high-growth company; as a result, it doesn't, by itself, make a company a venture-worthy investment.

If your aspiration is to raise venture capital, the primary question for new investors isn't when you can reach break-even. The primary questions are whether you're in a big market and how you can ramp growth (be it revenue or users) more aggressively to capture that market. Don't confuse the desire to raise money with the ability to spend it effectively.

Too Late for Hope, Too Early for Traction

At their core, investments are about opportunity and risk. How big is the opportunity, and how well is the company set up to capture it? What are the risks to capturing that opportunity, and how can they be mitigated? And, in the case of follow-on financings—those financings other than the first one—how much risk has been taken out since the previous financing?

Companies may ultimately raise numerous rounds of funding, both private and public. These rounds fall into three buckets, roughly paralleling the three stages of the Sales Learning Curve. If you find yourself stuck going more or less sideways a few years into building your company, understanding how startups are valued is key to understanding where you need to focus if you're to raise capital to grow your business. It's also an important consideration should you decide to sell instead, so you know how potential acquirers are likely to value your company.

People often bitterly complain about how seemingly arbitrary company valuations are. The markets reward consumer companies for user growth without meaningful revenue, while they typically measure business companies on revenue. Why is this the case? The simple answer is that the market values consumer and business startups very differently. Moreover, when it comes to acquisitions, external dynamics—such as an acquirer's need for a particular technology to fill a gap in their product line or strategy—can have a huge impact on a company's valuation.

Startups begin life with their value based on a combination of market demand for the deal, the pedigree of the team, and the potential market opportunity. Their founders sell the dream, and the companies are valued on hope. I recall the very first time I raised venture capital—I asked a potential investor how his firm had decided on the valuation for our company. Only half joking, he told me that because there were three of us, he estimated our individual values at about a million and a half dollars each and then threw in another half million because we were working together.

After the initial phase, companies go through a period of indeterminate value. They have some product and market traction, but they haven't taken out significant adoption risk. For the potential investor, the price of the investment may be significantly higher (based on management team expectations or market interest) but not priced commensurately with the lack of risk taken out of the investment.

Many have just enough traction that potential investors would rather wait until that traction is proven (and the associated risk taken out) than invest when no significant adoption risk has been removed. These startups are too late for hope but too early for traction.

Some companies go through repeated rounds of funding in this stage. Their traction curve is steepening, but the actual numbers are still too small or the curve too flat to change investor perception.

In the second stage, startups are valued on traction. For consumer companies, that means their ability to attract users, the number of those users, and the rate at which that number is growing. For the vast majority of business start-ups, it's the total size of the market opportunity and their revenue growth numbers in that market.

Consumer companies are valued differently because of the three M's:

- *Mass market:* Their markets are huge because potentially everyone on Earth could use their product.

- *Monetization:* All those users can consume ads, pay directly, or do both.

- *Main Street:* Many people have first-hand experience with the company's products or know about the company and are therefore more likely to want to buy the company's equity.

What's more, investors, from individuals to professionals, want to say they're in well-known, celebrity deals—they want hotness by association. The only question for these companies is whether they can get millions of consumers to use, and keep using, their product. When they can, they are, by definition, valuable, because relatively few companies are able to build something that millions of people want.

When it comes to getting out of the transition phase, your entire focus should be on changing the steepness of your traction curve. If you're building a consumer company, that means figuring out how to add users more quickly, and ideally reaching an exponential growth curve. If you're building a business-to-business company, it means changing the slope of your revenue curve—demonstrating that you can sell efficiently.

Are You Ready to Throw Gas on the Fire?

The Net Promoter Score[1] (NPS) measures the answer to the question: "How likely is it that you would recommend a company to a colleague or friend?" This is a great indicator of whether you're ready to throw gas on the fire.

The answer is given on a scale of one to ten, with respondents grouped into promoters, passives, and detractors. Companies with higher Net Promoter Scores have been shown to have faster, more efficient growth. Improving your score boils down to having more promoters and fewer detractors.

Companies with higher NPS values have more efficient growth engines because their customers are more likely to recommend their products to new customers. Not only is a high NPS a great indicator that customers like your product, but it also means they're providing you with free marketing! In addition to any marketing you do directly, a high NPS means you're leveraging your customers to help you acquire new ones—making your growth engine highly efficient.

Asking people whether they'd recommend your business to someone else is a lot different than simply asking them if they like your product. For one thing, people are often embarrassed to admit they don't like a product they bought—it makes them appear to have bad judgment. But to recommend that product to a friend, they really have to love it; few people want to be known to their friends or colleagues for recommending a bad product.

Putting NPS to work at your company doesn't mean you have to hire expensive consultants or spend a lot of money on surveys. It's easy to use tools like SurveyMonkey to ask your users or customers questions and tabulate the answers. And having a single metric like NPS is very useful—it's a straightforward measure you can watch over time.

A corollary to NPS is tracking how new customers find out about you. That way, you can invest more time and money in the channels that are working—and less in those that aren't. Tools like Google Analytics are important for tracking, but so is asking new users and customers, "How did you find out about us?"

If your NPS is high and you believe you have a big market opportunity—that is, the market is big, and a lot of other users or customers can derive the same

---

[1] Net Promoter is a registered trademark of Fred Reichheld, Bain & Company, described in his book, *The Ultimate Question*.

value as your existing base—then it's time to throw gas on the fire. Raise as much capital as you can, and invest in growth.

Get Out There and Sell

Even introverts who don't think of themselves as promoters are promoters. If you've ever raised a dime from someone else—be it a family member, a friend, or a professional investor—convinced a customer to buy your product or hear your pitch, or gotten someone to invest time working on your product in their off hours, you've been a promoter.

I used to think of sales in a very negative light. It was something other people did. I held onto that belief until I had to get out there and sell in order for my company to survive. I had to meet with customers, pitch investors, and recruit employees. It was humbling and exhilarating. Having had to sell my ideas, products, and companies over and over again, I now believe promotion is fundamental to the survival of any business—and you should, too.

When it comes to startups, *you* are just as much the product as your web site, software, or hardware. Potential users, customers, employees, and investors aren't just deciding to use your product—they're deciding to make an investment in you.

Some entrepreneurs mistakenly think that getting out there and promoting their products is something only non-tech-based companies need to do. After all, in an age where technology is everywhere, why would you need to have humans involved? This is a mistake.

There may have been a time when the Web was all about technology, but today's Web is all about being social—just look at Facebook and Twitter if you have any doubt. That means you need to be visible. As much as it might be nice if they did, products don't speak for themselves—entrepreneurs do. And with all the media available today—blogs, tweets, posts, not to mention numerous startup conferences that are always looking for entrepreneurs as speakers—there's no excuse not to be out there.

Being visible is no substitute for having a great product that people want to use and spend money on, or for working your way up the traction curve. But in an age when brand matters more than ever, raising your profile—if you do it in a positive way—can have innumerable benefits, from helping get you more users to helping you recruit employees and attract investment. Plus, being visible is incredibly cost-effective. It's a form of sales and marketing you can invest in without spending any financial capital.

Summary

Investing in sales and marketing too early can kill your company. It can burn up your hard-won cash. Yet not investing when you've got serious market traction can have equally disastrous effects. Although figuring out when you have the right amount of traction to invest more aggressively is very much an art, the tools presented in this chapter can add a little more science to your decision.

Failure comes from

- Investing in sales and marketing before you have product-market fit
- Insufficient experimentation
- Investing too late

It's time to spend on sales and marketing when

- You've found product-market fit.
- Users or customers are referring you to other customers.
- You're rapidly, measurably moving up the traction curve.

Losing Money on Sales

Put Sales Leverage to Work for You

Companies live or die on whether users invest with their time and customers invest with their wallets. We've all seen companies that spend more on every sale than they make. Their refrain, as the old joke goes, is, "We'll make it up in volume!"

It's funny to read about but no laughing matter when it's your own bank account. Rare is the entrepreneur who has profitable sales out of the gate. But the successful entrepreneur turns the model around and makes its scalable. A scalable sales model depends on sales that are profitable, repeatable, and efficient. Profitable, efficient sales come from knowing how much a customer or user is worth combined with a highly leveraged way to reach them. Repeatability comes from users or customers buying the same thing from you over and over again. How do you turn your sales model around and really make the engine hum?

When Customers Cost More Than They're Worth

Company M targeted small businesses with its content-hosting solution. The company acquired customers primarily through online advertising and search-engine optimization. I've changed the details, but the numbers are illustrative of the acquisition cost versus customer value challenge Company M faced.

Each month, the company spent about $21,000 on online advertising through Google AdWords. The company's cost per click (CPC) ranged from $3.73 to $4.56, with an average CPC of about $4.15. The company was able to convert around 1% of potential customers that clicked its ads, resulting in a cost per acquisition (CPA) of $415 per customer. (Out of 100 people who clicked at $4.15 per click, one converted to become a paying customer. Thus it cost $415 to acquire a customer.)

The founder of Company M was excited. He had found an acquisition channel that appeared to scale. He started spending.

Company M sold its product at multiple price points, but the most popular was its $19.95 per month Bronze offering. At that price, it would take about 21 months for the company to break even on its CPA. The company would have to lay out $415 up front and wait 21 months before it started making a profit on that customer—and that was to cover its marketing costs, not taking into account other costs such as hosting and customer support. What's more, each customer would have to continue using Company M's product for more than 21 months—if any churned out, Company M would lose money.

Some customers did churn out. In fact, some 20% of Company M's customers churned out—many liked the product, but, being small businesses, they simply went out of business.

After more than a year of spending, watching his customer churn rates, and managing down the CPA, the founder of Company M realized the two lines—his CPA and his customer lifetime value (CLV) weren't going to converge quickly enough. He laid off most of his staff and reduced his marketing spend. Only time will tell whether he can rebuild the business.

Ultimately, It's About Acquisition

If you can't acquire users or customers profitably and repeatedly, you may be able to survive for a long time on capital from investors, but ultimately you can't build a sustainable business. Frankly, as heretical as it may sound, you may be able to make a lot of money building an unprofitable business. Many entrepreneurs and investors have made plenty of money building businesses that lost money hand over first and weren't sustainable.

That's because when it comes to tech companies, the capital markets tend to reward growth, and sometimes even just the potential for growth, over profitability. Alternatively, a startup that is unprofitable may be profitable when rolled into a larger company that has a more efficient way to reach the market. Or a larger company may simply want to acquire a startup for its people or technology, netting the founders and investors a handsome profit in the process.

Of course, far more of these unprofitable companies go out of business along the way. If you want to build a sustainable business or control your own destiny, you have to figure out how your company can make money. Making money requires you to acquire users profitably. Simply put, that means monetizing users or customers for more than it costs you to acquire and serve them.

Understand Customer Lifetime Value

CLV measures how much revenue a customer generates over the time they remain a customer of your company. Revenue can come directly from the customer, but it can also come from third parties; this is common for businesses that monetize via advertising. By determining CLV across a number of customers, you can figure out how much you can afford to spend to acquire a customer.

For example, if a customer is expected to generate $100 in revenue over their lifetime, you can in theory spend up to $99.99 to acquire and serve that customer and still be profitable on each customer. Of course, you're generating only one cent in profit for every customer! That likely isn't enough to pay for all your other costs—your own salary, that of your management team, and the costs of software development, for example.

However, if it costs you $10 to acquire and serve a customer, and you can monetize that customer for $100, you make $90: a far more appealing proposition. That should be more than enough to cover all your other costs and leave you with a nice profit.

What if you have to spend the $10 up front, but you collect only $1 each year for 10 years? That situation creates a cashflow problem. That is, you don't have enough cash to spend on acquiring new customers because you're being paid back far too slowly. Clearly, to become a profitable company, you must not only be able to acquire customers profitably but also do so in a timeframe that supports your cashflow requirements and growth objectives.

When companies start out, the amount they spend to acquire a customer often far exceeds the amount for which they can monetize that customer. That is the nature of new companies—while they're figuring out the most efficient way to acquire customers, every new customer is a learning experience. That learning is expensive but pays back its cost many times when you determine how to acquire customers or users in a repeatable and scalable manner.

Many startups get trapped in continuing to invest large amounts in customer acquisition, only to discover that they can't get the cost of acquisition down. Every "sale"—that is, a new user or a new paying customer—is a one-off. These companies are unable to move from learning to scalable execution.

Churn is another common challenge that companies face. When companies have high churn, it means customers or users are showing up to use the product—and then going away. Having high churn is like trying to fish with a sieve: you may occasionally catch a fish, but most of them swim on through.

If you have high churn, it may appear that your company is growing rapidly, especially if you can generate new users or customers more quickly than you lose them. But because those new users don't stick around, you're fighting a constant battle; ultimately, your apparent growth falls off, and you haven't built a growth engine that can truly scale.

Users and customers leave for a variety of reasons. If you're selling to small businesses, given their high failure rates, a lot of them simply go out of business. If you're building a consumer product, users may like the promise of your offering, but once they try it, see no reason to continue using it. You're failing to engage your users, so you can't retain them.

And in all cases, if you don't have a compelling and sticky offering—an offering that locks in the customer and makes it hard to switch while solving the customer's needs—a competitor can swoop in and take your customers. In that case, you're spending a lot of marketing and sales dollars educating customers, only to have someone else monetize them.

Remember: Products Are Bought, Not Sold

People are fond of talking about selling, but really we should all talk about buying. That's because your product is bought, not sold. Of course, you've probably let yourself be talked into buying something you didn't need or made an impulse purchase because an item seemed like a good deal. But when it comes to the very best products, people *want* to buy them.

Consider the lines in front of Apple Stores the day before a new iPhone goes on sale. Think about concerts that are so popular they not only sell out but have scalpers selling tickets for far more than they originally cost. Or recall the last time you tried to go on vacation during a holiday season, and the associated cost of airfare and hotel rooms.

What do all these products have in common? They're in demand, and they're scarce. Scarcity and demand obviously go hand in hand. More often than not, they don't come about naturally: they must be created. This is why so much marketing today refers to *demand generation* rather than sales.

Certainly, the sales pitch, nowhere more artfully demonstrated than in episodes of *Mad Men*, still exists. But with the amount of information now available on the Internet, transparency around price and quality has increased significantly. From sites like Yelp and TripAdvisor for restaurant and hotel reviews to Amazon for product reviews, information about products is widely available. As a result, great products are a must.

So is demand creation—because if your product seems undifferentiated, people will simply go for the lowest price. And there are many ways to differentiate—from the product itself to how you position and deliver it. Great service is a differentiator too.

Fight Inherent Bias

Ask an enterprise sales executive how they would solve a sales-execution problem, and the answer will most likely be, "Put in place a sales methodology, set a quota, and hire the right sales people."

Ask a product person how they would solve a sales problem, and the answer will most likely be, "Remove any friction in the way of product adoption, and make it easier to buy."

Ask someone who's been 100% focused on online marketing, and the answer may well be, "Spend money on Google AdWords and a variety of other online lead-generation mechanisms."

Ask a consumer Internet entrepreneur, and the answer will be, "Go viral."

Which of these answers is correct? They all are—from the point of view of the person answering the question! They may not be the right answer for your startup, however. The issue you face is that people bring inherent biases with them. They tend to go with what they know and with what has worked for them in the past. Big enterprise sales execs go with big enterprise sales models. Online marketers go with online marketing. Those who have built brands for big companies in the past want to spend lots of money on marketing and brand building.

Everyone is susceptible to this kind of bias—even your most experienced board members. They may be the most susceptible, because they're using pattern matching as the basis for their advice based on companies they previously invested in that worked (or didn't work).

But what worked in the past may have depended as much on a particular market or market conditions as on the startup itself. What's more, if you push someone to market and sell in a way that's not natural to them—say, suggesting that an enterprise sales executive market and sell only via a light-touch Internet approach—you set up that person to fail.

How do you fight bias like this? Although it's difficult, the best solution is to *look at the data*. But realistically, no matter how much you do that, you'll probably turn over your sales team a few times before you get one in place that works. It may feel like a bad thing when it's happening—and it certainly feels painful to the organization—but it's the nature of a startup's evolution.

Reduce Sales Team Turnover

It's almost a given that in every startup, sales executives are turned over more than just about anyone else in the company. That was the case with Company X, which went through three VPs of sales in 12 months. The first head of sales was a channel executive who knew a lot about setting up partnerships but very little about running an actual sales organization and "owning the number." He lasted almost two quarters before the board leaned on the CEO to fire the exec and get someone more familiar with direct sales.

The second head of sales was the real deal. He had a track record of helping companies grow from the low millions of dollars in revenue to $50 million, $80 million, and over $100 million in revenue. Sales model *discovery* followed by scaling was his sweet spot. He didn't enjoy working in really big organizations, but he did enjoy tuning the sales model and then putting a team in place to execute on it.

Although Company X was, as he put it, "a little earlier" than he was used to, he joined because a good friend of his was on the board and encouraged him to take the job. He was at one board meeting and gone before the next. A savvy individual, he quickly figured out that the company wasn't a little earlier than he was used to—it was a lot earlier. In fact, Company X was still a long way from finding product-market fit. Of course, the CEO of Company X blamed the sales executive, saying he had turned out not to be a good fit for the company.

The third sales executive went through a number of lengthy interviews with the board members, all of whom had previous operating experience. Having been through two sales executives in rapid succession, neither the CEO nor the board was eager to hire another mismatched executive. The decision to hire the third sales executive was unanimous—as was the decision to make him CEO a few months later.

He came right out and said the one thing no one else had been willing to: it wasn't a question of sales execution that was killing the company. It was a lack of product-market fit. While other companies in the space were having great success, Company X continued to struggle. Perhaps the third sales exec had more on the line than the second one, or perhaps he wanted to prove he could make it work—as CEO. Given the choice between him becoming CEO and losing sales executive number three, the board decided to make him CEO.

Failing fast is one mark of a great startup. But making the same mistake repeatedly isn't. Don't hire senior executives and staff up before you're ready for them. Doing so just wastes time and capital. And, as I talked about in the last chapter, great sales operations are no substitute for product-market fit.

Get Sales Leverage

Sales leverage is all about reaching customers efficiently. Pivoting doesn't just apply to your product strategy; it also applies to your go-to-market strategy. If you feel you have product-market fit, but you're not reaching your potential customers and your business isn't growing the way you want it to, it's time to pivot your model.

The Traditional Way

The most cost-effective way to get new customers or users, of course, is for your existing customers or users to recruit them for you.

Historically, companies run advertisements, do PR campaigns, and then put "feet on the street" to sell their products. Drug company representatives go door to door to meet with doctors and educate them about new products.

Traditional software companies have account executives (AEs) who meet with big customers in person. Sales engineers (SEs) then install the software and perform any configuration—and sometimes, costly customization—of the software for the customer's environment. Some software products are so complex or need to be customized to such an extent that the customer pays professional service fees on top of the cost of the base product. Teams from the software maker itself or from a third party install and customize the software.

Enter the Cloud

Today, most software is in the cloud. This means instead of the product being installed on premises—that is, on the customer's servers at the customer's location—and managed by the customer's employees or a designated third party, the software is run at a data center external to the customer. The vendor manages and updates the software. Although this model existed before Salesforce.com, that company was the first to make Software as a Service (SaaS), software delivered via the cloud, a widely accepted practice.

Delivering software this way has transformed the way software is sold, enabling a variety of innovative new business models.

The Freemium Model

Well-known tech companies like Dropbox, Evernote, LinkedIn, Skype, and others have implemented the freemium model with much success, and you can too. In this model, a company gives away the basic product for free and then charges for premium services.

Business-to-business (B2B) companies are using this innovative model to disrupt classic business software models. With freemium, your customers don't pay you up front—they get to try the product for free. The idea is to get them hooked, so that they decide to pay to keep using the product or to take advantage of premium features.

To be clear, the freemium model comes in two flavors. In one case, customers get to use the complete product free of charge during the trial period, and then they must convert to paid to continue their usage. In the second case, your base product (perhaps a personal edition to be used by one or two users only) is free, but customers pay for premium features or higher-end packages that include business capabilities like more storage, more email, or multiple-user support.

The freemium model itself isn't new—shareware programs of the 1980s and 1990s used a similar model, where customers could use the product for free and then pay if they wanted to continue to use the app. These applications came in the form of installed software, with the user bearing any associated computing and storage costs. With hosted, web-based services, the costs of bandwidth, storage, and processing are borne by the company. Historically, this was expensive, and it meant that supporting a user for free was equally expensive, preventing freemium from being a viable approach for hosted services.

But the decline in the costs of these infrastructure services, and the ability to rely on them being delivered by Amazon Web Services, for example, means that the incremental cost of supporting an additional user is very low. As a result, many companies have been able to implement the freemium model successfully. They can afford to take on new users for free, and they view the costs of supporting such users as their marketing cost—and frequently that's a lot more cost-effective than paid marketing.

Although the model can be used for all kinds of services, it's especially useful when users create or upload their own content, as is the case with Dropbox, Evernote, and others. Once users upload their content, they want ongoing access to it. This makes them more likely to convert to paying customers and stick around, because although it's possible for them to switch to another service, transferring their content requires a significant investment of time and energy.

The risk with freemium is that customers may decide your product is nice to use if it's free but not worth paying for if it isn't. You may end up with tons of users using the free version of your service but have limited success converting them to paying customers. Users who abuse the service or fail to convert cost you money and hurt your margins. Supporting them also costs time and money. If there are too many of them, you have implemented the *dreamium* model, not freemium.

Given that freemium plans typically see a conversion rate of 1% to 5% from free to paid (with 5% being incredibly high), you must have *a lot* of users for freemium to work. Looking at Evernote, Dropbox, LinkedIn, and others, the common theme is that they all have *millions, if not tens of millions of users*.

Their products appeal to a very broad base of potential users, who are all signing up for their products individually. Although businesses or employees may ultimately pay for products like LinkedIn and Dropbox, it's millions of individuals who sign up for the service. If your service doesn't potentially appeal to millions of individuals, freemium probably won't work for you. It may look good at the outset, but there won't be enough users for it to work at scale. In that case, you should turn off your free option and charge for your product.

Zero-Cost User Acquisition

Pioneered by consumer Internet companies, especially social networks like Facebook, zero-cost user acquisition is literally just that: it costs nothing to acquire another user. It's the most highly leveraged and efficient model of all.

Zero-cost user acquisition is easiest when your users are your content—their pictures, words, files, and activities are what make your product what it is. Your product provides the framework for them, but they (and their associated digital media and actions) are the content.

The more your users are the content, and the more the benefit of the product is a result of them sharing their content and actions with others, the closer you are to zero-cost user acquisition. That's because your users will naturally want to invite friends and colleagues to the site, because the more friends and colleagues are on the site, the more benefit the original inviter derives from the service.

Word of Mouth

But you don't have to be building a social network to implement some of the approaches of zero-cost user acquisition. Zero-cost user acquisition also comes in the form of word of mouth. This is perhaps one of the most powerful forms of marketing (and sales) ever.

Consider online shoe seller Zappos, known for its excellent customer service. Other companies sold shoes on the Web for years before Zappos showed up. But Zappos introduced free two-way shipping and incredible customer service. Customers loved it—they reviewed the company positively online, and they told their friends. Word spread like wildfire, and Zappos became so successful that it was acquired by Amazon for more than a billion dollars.

Of course, Zappos spent money on advertising. But more important, the company became known for one thing: its industry-leading customer service. People loved talking about their Zappos' experience. By developing a *reputation* for doing one thing—customer service—better than any other company, Zappos revolutionized its category and became successful through word of mouth.

Figure out the one thing you can be better at than any other company in your category, become known for that, and you can put word of mouth to work to grow your business, too.

Partnering

One often overlooked path to sales leverage is via partnering with a larger company that already has an efficient channel to the market. Of course, this approach comes at a cost: partnerships are notoriously difficult to come by, plus you give up a portion of your revenue to the partner.

The risk with partnering is that you become so dependent on the partner that you can't acquire customers without them. But some companies and their platforms have so much reach that paying them the tax to acquire customers may well be more effective than trying to acquire those customers directly.

Many companies are acquiring users by developing mobile applications and listing them in the Apple App Store or working with partners like Salesforce.com that already have large and efficient customer reach. When you consider that ultimately you need to spend money on customer acquisition one way or another, these kinds of relationships can be an important component of a broader acquisition strategy.

Repeatedly Monetizing Your Users

One of the best sources of revenue you can come by is revenue from existing users. If someone is using your product, you've already paid the cost to acquire them. As a result, any more money you can get them to spend with you is revenue that goes straight to your bottom line.

This is called *farming* your existing user base. The reality is, existing, satisfied users *want* to spend more money with you! You just have to give them a way to do so. You can upsell them on a more expensive offering, sell them new features, or charge them for usage (of storage, for example). Or, in the case of ad-supported businesses, you can get them to spend more time on your site, which should result in them seeing, and ultimately clicking, more ads.

Of course, it's also possible to over-monetize your users. Web sites that put too many ads in front of their users, for example, can detract from the core user experience. Social network MySpace suffered from ad burnout—users of the site saw so many ads that they tuned them out. Finding the right balance is key.

Making the Engine Hum

There are plenty of tactical items that, when all put together, can clog up a sales engine. Ineffective sales people, bad contracts, pricing that's a complete mismatch for the value customers perceive they're getting, lack of good process, and a sales funnel that acts more like a leaky bucket can all destroy sales execution. Let's take them in order.

Ineffective Sales People

Ineffective sales people are a form of lack of product-market fit. Instead of the product being your actual product, the product is the sales person, and the market is the individual customer looking to make a purchase. I recall a sales team where calls were routed randomly to the inside sales representatives. They didn't get to choose which customers they talked to; they simply picked up the phone when it rang. Yet in one month, the best performer sold five times more than the worst performer.

The CEO, who was new to managing a larger sales operation, figured that his VP of sales could coach the worst performers to do better. The company and the worst performers both invested many months, yet the resulting improvement was minimal. Ultimately the CEO decided to focus the company on its strengths.

After moving the VP of Sales to another role and taking over the job himself, the CEO laid off his worst-performing sales people and hired more people like those who were successful. The strategy worked—and the rest of the organization was overjoyed. Having the non-performers on the team for so long had started to take its toll and demoralize the other employees.

Bad Contracts

Bad contracts can limit a company's upside and cost you a lot of money. Pressured to get deals done by its board, Company Z cut sweetheart deals with its customers. Although the deals looked great on paper, they restricted Company Z's ability to get more revenue from the customers as the company expanded its product's reach in its customers' organizations. You often need to discount aggressively to get early customers. But contractually limiting your upside can come back to bite you later.

Painful as it was, ultimately Company Z had to go back to these customers and tell them it couldn't afford to service them as customers under the agreed-on contracts. Some customers reacted very negatively. Many, however, responded with, "We couldn't understand how you could afford to charge us this little." Were they happy about renegotiating? Certainly not. But they needed the product enough that they didn't want Company Z to go out of business.

Mismatched Pricing

Pricing that is a mismatch with a customer's expectation of value can also kill a company. This frequently happens when startups introduce products that compete with those from larger companies. I have heard the refrain, "But [big company X] charges tens of thousands of dollars for a product like ours, and our product is a lot better" more times than I care to remember. Yes—but you're not big company X.

Bad Sales Process

Bad sales process and a leaky funnel go hand in hand. Many startups have potential customers or users coming in that they aren't taking care of. In an ideal world, every sale would be a self-serve sale. Customers would come to your web site, put in their payment info, and buy your product. Or, in the case of a consumer web site, they would register and become ongoing, active users. The reality is often quite different.

Hard as it may be to believe, your site may make it too difficult for customers to sign up and pay you. Customers may have questions about your product because you haven't refined the information on your site to the point that they can find the answers. Or, they may want to speak to, chat with, or email a human being just to make sure you're "real." This is especially true in the early days of a startup.

The bad news about a clogged engine is that missed opportunities may be chewing up your potential profits—and your reputation, if word spreads that you're unresponsive to your customers.

The good news is that you can solve the leaky-bucket problem with data and attention to process. For web sites, you can instrument your site and know exactly how many people who come to the site convert into leads and paying customers. Consumer companies can track how many users turn into registered users and then remain as active users. They can figure out the specific actions taken by users who stick around, and then focus on getting more new users to perform those same activities.

Summary

Pivoting doesn't just apply to your product strategy. It applies to your go-to-market strategy too. Keep refining your go-to-market strategy until you have a highly leveraged model:

- Develop a reputation for being better at one thing than any other company in your category.

- Use innovative new sales models to accelerate your growth.

- Figure out how much your users or customers are worth to you, and then run the numbers to determine how much you can spend to acquire and serve them.

- Sales team turnover is a natural part of company evolution.

Invisible Startups

Market Your Startup Without Incinerating Cash

So you've got a great market and a great product. A few select people know about your product, they use it all the time, and they love it. Problem is, they're all friends of yours! Like the tree falling in the empty forest, thousands of great products have gone unused because no one knew they existed. You're not just unknown—you're invisible.

But how do you get the word out in a crowded market? How do you stand out from the crowd without mortgaging your house or burning through your hard-won venture dollars? No longer is it sufficient to do basic search-engine marketing and optimization. Just buying keywords, putting up landing pages on your web site, and doing PR won't cut it. Avoid getting lost in the noise and stand out from the crowd using these seven proven ways to market your startup.

Startups You've Never Heard Of

Investors lump failures into one of two categories.

Some companies struggle in a market where everyone fails. Things look good, but ultimately mainstream customers or a large volume of users are unwilling to take a chance on a new concept. Skilled execution and a reasonable backup plan don't compensate for a market that fails to develop as quickly as originally anticipated. Some entrepreneurs are able to switch markets completely early on—if they haven't raised and spent too much cash. But typically in this scenario, all companies in the given market flounder or fail. It isn't a desired outcome, but it's not for lack of trying. It's often the nature of creating new markets.

Then there are the really painful failures—those that keep me and other investors I know up at night. Some investments fail due to self-inflicted wounds. A competitor winds up owning what turns out to be a very large market. The other company moved faster and out-executed. Often, they did this by having a better product *and* by out-acquiring users or customers. Here's a good example.

The file-sharing market has existed for a long time. For as long as computers have been around, people have needed to move files from one place to another. Yet we've all experienced attaching a large file to an e-mail message only to find out that the file was too big to send or get a bounce-back message indicating it was too large for the recipient to receive. And the problem has only gotten worse as people have started creating, capturing, and sharing more and more high-resolution media.

From product-design files to project documents, from high-resolution photographs to video, everyone needs to move more and bigger files, and share them not just with one person but with friends and large teams. Although high-speed broadband seems as though it could have made this problem virtually disappear, it's had the opposite effect—now that many people have a high-speed connection, they expect to be able to move large files quickly and easily. They often need to share media with others or want to back up all those documents, videos, photographs, and other important files.

Recognizing the increased adoption of high-speed broadband and the creation of larger files, a number of companies developed file-sharing products early on. But they faced some significant challenges to adoption.

Some of the companies were simply too early to market. People had relatively high-speed Internet, but it wasn't yet fast enough to support rapid transfer of large files. It might be okay for an upload to go on for hours or days in the background, but if took that long to retrieve a file, forget it. What's more, storage and bandwidth costs were prohibitively high—the companies couldn't offer storage at a price that customers were willing to accept and still make money. They failed because they were too early.

Later, the gorillas entered the market—Amazon, Apple, Google, and Microsoft—primarily by acquiring companies in the space, integrating, and rebranding their products. Yet all the gorilla and stand-alone product offerings had critical shortcomings: restrictions on uploading or sharing of larger files, really slow upload speeds, and/or hard-to-use user interfaces.

Some lacked a desktop component, so users had to drop large files onto a browser and then leave the browser window open while waiting for the upload to complete—which could take hours and made it very difficult to synchronize files across different devices. These products failed because they weren't great products and they didn't live up to users' expectations.

Enter the cloud. Lots of products existed in the space, but none truly solved the problem: making it easy to share and synchronize files across any device, privately or with others. Two companies emerged as the market leaders: Box.net and Dropbox. Box targeted the enterprise, and Dropbox the consumer.

These companies did two things well that differentiated them from the failures. They built exceptionally easy-to-use products that solved the problem and "just worked," and they transformed the way file-sharing products were marketed. In doing so, they transformed the market.

Instead of talking about file sharing or backup or moving bits around, they talked about access on any device. They talked about simplicity. They talked about transforming your data. And it wasn't just talk; their products matched their marketing promise.

In fact, they became marketing machines. They used many of the tactics described in this chapter to become the well-known technology leaders they are today. So can you.

Product Innovation

Product innovation may be your best marketing and acquisition strategy.

The number-one factor in marketing success is a great product. Deliver a bad product, and people will write and talk about it. Today, there is no hiding from bad product. Customers don't just call customer service to complain—they post, tweet, and create YouTube videos like the well-known "United Breaks Guitars."

A great product is one that is easy to use, is self-explanatory, and delights your customers and users. Apple has a great brand because the company has combined best-of-breed product with brilliant marketing. Fundamentally, the company's products are intuitive, well designed, and pleasing to the user from start to finish. From purchasing to unwrapping to using to doing more purchasing, Apple delivers an excellent user experience.

What's more, Apple's products grow with you. A new iPad user might not realize that swiping left brings up search, but over time they figure it out. Seemingly small things like making more advanced features discoverable provide a great experience. But they also incent users with a reward: that "ah hah" moment when they discover a new feature themselves, which in turn releases dopamine, a chemical that controls the brain's pleasure and reward systems.

Product matters more now than ever before. The Internet has increased the speed at which word of mouth spreads. Entrepreneurs are creating new products at unprecedented rates due to the declining cost and broader availability of infrastructure needed to build and deliver products to market. This means consumers and business users alike have more alternatives.

Design matters more now than does technology alone. Information technology has achieved mass adoption. Even the most technology-resistant people now text, check e-mail, and browse the Web at home, at work, and on their phones. It's no longer sufficient just to build a product of features.

It used to be so fundamentally difficult to build product that vast amounts of engineering time and capital were consumed getting the product to work. Nearly everything had to be built from scratch. Today, however, you can leverage a lot of existing building blocks; and, just as critically, you can get your product into the hands of potential users for feedback much more quickly and easily.

That doesn't mean all the hard technology problems have been solved, nor that products must be perfect before you release them to the market. But it does mean you can't just cough up new products and expect users to use them. New products must have the design, integration, and ease of use today's savvy consumers have come to expect.

More products are becoming platforms. Some of the most interesting product innovations don't come from your own product team but from other people leveraging your product as a platform. Of note in recent years was social gaming company Zynga's ability to tap into the inherent virality of Facebook to expand its user base rapidly.

Opening up your product to integration with others not only drives faster adoption but also spurs new innovations. In the past, only the very largest companies could be platforms—Apple and Microsoft, for example. Because many applications are now delivered over the Web, however, opening up an interface that allows third party developers to integrate with your product is not only straightforward, it's expected.

That said, with rare exceptions, products come first, and platforms come second. Companies ultimately recognized as platforms don't typically start out building platforms—they build applications that gain widespread adoption first, and then they open up to become platforms. Amazon, Salesforce, Facebook, Google, and others that have emerged to become platform companies, were successful as application companies first.

But opening yourself up and defining yourself as a platform—once you've achieved application success, of course—does one other incredible thing for you from a marketing perspective: it puts you in the center of the ecosystem rather than on the edge of the circle. That means you get to define your market position rather than have others define it for you. It puts you at the center of activity rather than at the periphery. The more you define your ecosystem, the more control you have over your own destiny—a good thing for any startup.

Viral Marketing

To make your product viral, make viral your product. Imagine Facebook or YouTube without user-uploaded photos and videos and the ability to share them easily. Unlike other marketing techniques, viral is built-in and free. With viral acquisition, your users acquire you more users just by using your product.

Some products are inherently viral—Facebook and LinkedIn, for example. At their core, they're frameworks for letting people share their own content. In the case of Facebook, that's personal content like photos and updates on what people are up to. In the case of LinkedIn, it's professional networking information.

Not all products are naturally viral from the ground up, but by giving your users the ability to invite their friends, make money, get a discount, or obtain capabilities such as free storage for every user they refer, your site or app can take advantage of viral marketing. You can go one step further by adding special features only available to those who get their friends to sign up. Viral marketing, executed well, delivers near zero-cost user acquisition. A big part of that efficiency is that viral marketing leverages existing user-acquisition and communication mechanisms like e-mail and social networks.

One compelling form of viral marketing is media sharing. If your product requires users to share what they're doing (documents, images, or links, for example) with others, that drives adoption. Every time an existing user shares a piece of media with a friend or colleague, your product has been exposed to a potential new user.

Part of what makes viral adoption work so well is its personalized nature. As Robert Cialdini pointed out in *Influence: The Psychology of Persuasion* (Harper, 2006), people trust recommendations from those they already trust. So when your friend Joe says he's using a new application and suggests you use it too, that's likely to carry more weight than randomly hearing about the application. Although you may not be able to turn your application into a viral-content container like Facebook or LinkedIn, you can certainly incorporate some basic viral elements along these lines. "Joe is using Application X," and "Joe shared a document with you," both carry a lot of weight because they're coming from a trusted source—Joe.

Nearly every product today should have at least the most basic of viral elements built in. Ideally, it should also incorporate virality in a much more fundamental way into core product design so that it uses e-mail, social networks, and other mechanisms to get the word out.

Hand in hand with building in viral features, of course, is testing their impact and making changes based on the data. Everything about a viral feature can be measured, tested, and iterated on, from senders to receivers to the content of the message itself. For example, what are the characteristics of senders whose invites are most frequently accepted? How about those of recipients who accept invitations? What about the content of the invitation?

Users and potential users provide huge amounts of *signaling data* through their actions—you can make this data actionable by measuring it.

Viral marketing works best when coupled with gaming dynamics. File-sharing company Dropbox calls its free space a *bonus*. It's not just free space: "You're 2 steps away from a 250MB bonus." And it couples that with *quests*, much like a game: "Complete these quests and become a Dropbox guru!"

The product seamlessly introduces rewards in the form of bonuses, quests to complete, and status levels like guru. These incent user behavior and drive adoption. They also make the product fun, adding excitement to potentially mundane steps like putting files in a folder and installing an application on your mobile device.

Social Media

People often lump viral marketing and social media together. In reality, viral marketing and social media are very different. Social media (or *social*) can help get the viral-marketing flywheel spinning, but at its core, social is about presence, credibility, and visibility.

Social is pages, likes, tweets, posts, blogs, answers, comments, and word of mouth. Inexpensive e-mail newsletter tools are available to help you communicate with users, and they can be a very effective way to re-engage those who have tried your product in the past. You can bring social directly into your application by combining viral and social, social and mobile. More on that later.

Fortunately, it's easy to use social media these days. Post regularly on your site's blog. Tweet about new features, customers, and users multiple times per day. Social means being part of the conversation. So don't just do it yourself—enlist your customers, fans, and friends to leave comments, write, and tweet about you and your products.

Create videos and podcasts, and publish those on your web site as well as on destinations like YouTube and other web sites. This is an excellent and low-cost form of marketing that takes advantage of the great asset you have in your users and customers. Don't just make the videos about your product—enlist your users and customers to make the content more personal and applicable.

You can also create online communities for your users. Not only a community for discussion or help about your product—although that is certainly a must—but also a destination where users can share their stories and connect emotionally with you and your product.

Consider a company that provides web-based customer-support software. Although the product itself may not be viral, the company can create a social destination, something like CustomerServicesReallySuck.com[1]. Everyone has had a bad customer-service experience at one time or another and wanted to share their pain and frustration by telling someone else about that experience. A web-based customer support company can easily tap into that pent-up customer anguish by providing an outlet for it—and, of course, the solution.

What do you do if you're bootstrapped and find yourself without the time (or interest) to tweet, blog, and comment? Either make the time or do what many

---

[1] A name used for illustrative purposes.

other companies do: hire someone to do these activities for you. Think you can't afford to? The real question is whether you can afford *not* to. Plus, with recent college graduate unemployment rates at their highest in decades, you should be able to find someone highly educated and Internet savvy who is looking for experience and income. Put that person to work as your social media expert.

Buzz

Closely related to social is buzz. *Buzz* means your company is visible—highly visible. To get buzz, you need to take advantage of that other four-letter word, *hype*. To generate buzz, it's not enough to tweet, post, and blog. You have to be visible: on Internet TV shows, in blogs, at big events. You have to be seen as a leader in your space, often slightly controversial or edgy. Get people talking about your company, your product, or you. Today, success begets visibility, and visibility begets success.

I grew up in the school of thought best articulated by Steve Jobs in 2003: "Our belief was that if we kept putting great products in front of customers, they would continue to open their wallets." I still agree with that statement. But don't forget the 1984 Apple Super Bowl commercial: not only did it create buzz, but it also created an emotional connection. Fortunately, these days, you don't need to spend millions of dollars on a Super Bowl ad to generate buzz.

Prior to the late 1990s, few had heard of an individual who had been a vice president at Bankers Trust and a computer scientist at D. E. Shaw & Co. This individual went on to make the—at the time—outrageous claim that he was building the world's largest bookstore. Of course, everyone now knows the name Jeff Bezos and the company Amazon.com.

Being unique, social, and personally visible is critical to generating buzz. But it's not sufficient. To stand out from the masses, you must go one step further. You must have and communicate a transformative vision, also known as a BHAG—a Big Hairy Audacious Goal—coined by Jim Collins and Jerry Porras in their book *Good to Great* (HarperBusiness, 2001).

Some may consider BHAG a cliché. After all, what startup really needs to deal with things like vision and mission? But consider the difference between "a set of web pages for displaying customer information stored in a database" and "the end of software." Both statements describe the world's largest customer relationship management (CRM) company, Salesforce.com. But it's clear which statement is more proactive, visionary, and buzz-worthy.

To be worthwhile, buzz must translate into value. In its most extreme form, buzz may appear purely superficial. But not only did "the end of software" statement serve Salesforce.com's marketing purposes, it also served as a clear point of differentiation, a focus, and as a rallying cry for the company.

Done right, buzz is more than skin deep. It's the articulation of a vision that comes from your company's very core. That helps you sell product, drives user awareness, and helps with financing activities and, ultimately, liquidity. Moreover, in crowded spaces, a big, transformative vision combined with a powerful articulation of that vision lets one company break out from the pack.

Search

With Facebook accounting for some 25% of U.S. Internet traffic, it might be tempting to discount traditional online acquisition mechanisms such as search. But search, in the form of search engine optimization (SEO)[2] and search engine marketing (SEM), generates a lot of users. According to some estimates, Google handles about three billion searches per day. The challenge is making search cost-effective as a way for your company to acquire customers. With patience, effort, and the right analytics tools, however, search pays off.

Test, measure, and repeat. Nothing is too small to be tested, from pricing plans and ad copy to layouts, colors, and animated buttons. Ask every customer to link back to you from their web site—consider offering discounts to those that do. Not all of them will do it, but enough will to drive up your rankings and traffic. Get the details right, such as anchor text, so you rank high in search results for the terms you care about. Plus, referral traffic alone boosts sales. Add an affiliate program to reward your customers and partners for sending people your way.

Defining your goals and tuning your conversion flow before spending too much money is critical. The right product-market fit—a product and price point that

---

[2] Search engine optimization (SEO) is the practice of optimizing the content on your web site and the inbound links from other sites pointing to your site to increase your ranking in a search engine. Search engine marketing (SEM) deals with managing the advertisements displayed above and to the side of Google search results and on sites that display Google-served ads.

a very large number of people want—is paramount. When it comes to search marketing, the sheer volume of searches means it's easy to spend a lot of money and produce very little in the way of results.

Company X decided to invest in Google AdWords as a way to acquire customers. However, the company didn't define goals for the campaigns ahead of time, nor did it give much thought to the rest of the flow, such as landing pages and what to do when customers indicated their interest. This may seem unfathomable—why spend money before you know what you plan to do with the results? But it happens in startups all the time.

In contrast, Company Y, which was targeting small and medium businesses (SMBs), set clear goals for its online marketing campaigns and was even showing good progress—but it couldn't find a path from generating a few customers a day to generating thousands of them. This is mission-critical in the SMB space. So although it won the battle on AdWords, it lost the war on scaling the overall business.

Company Z was very successful at buying AdWords that converted people into customers, but it had a leaky-bucket problem. Customers came, tried the product, and then left. It appeared for a period of time that the company was making progress, but it wasn't. The company had found half of the product-market equation: the market. But it hadn't yet discovered product fit for that market; users either weren't getting what they expected or weren't getting enough value. Either way, they weren't sticking around.

The management of Company Z, feeling pressure to grow, continued to spend without pausing to refine the product. The decision to keep spending seemed like the right one—customer acquisition appeared to be working. Yet the team didn't want to admit that half the equation wasn't right and adjust course accordingly.

If any of these sounds like your business, then before spending another penny on online marketing, ask yourself two questions. First, what is your online marketing goal? It's most likely not one goal but a series of milestones. It's fine for your first goal to be, for example, "Let's learn whether we can acquire customers via AdWords." The next goal might be, "Let's determine the cost of acquisition and whether it will be profitable for us." And finally, "How much can we spend, and how fast?" In other words, get a sense of whether a particular acquisition channel will work at all, and then refine and optimize. Second, keep asking yourself whether you have product-market fit—are you able to get customers to come to the well (market) and to keep drinking from it (product)?

Finally, there are some very low-cost yet innovative ways to drive search (and word of mouth) traffic. One example is to create compelling content to which people want to refer. Infographics are a great way to do this. With relatively little effort, crowd-sourced work company oDesk created such a graphic to represent reaching more than one million hours of work done per month. Numerous people linked back to, commented on, and shared the graphic because it provided interesting data in an informative and unique format. The result was more links back to the company's web site, which both improved the site's rankings in search results and drove traffic directly to the site.

Mobile

According to an article in the *New York Times*, the average smartphone user spends 667 minutes each month using mobile apps.[3] That's more time than those users spend talking on the phone. To reach your potential users where they are, you need to have a strong mobile presence.

Plus, many compelling features are only enabled on mobile: photos and video on the go and, of course, location. In addition to providing great marketing, developing a mobile version of your application is sure to be a great source of product innovation, as your users unlock new and exciting use cases for your product, leading to new market and revenue opportunities for your company.

Of course, some applications are mobile in and of themselves. The primary use case for photo apps, video apps, and many games is a mobile one. Other applications aren't inherently mobile or weren't originally designed to be mobile but have added compelling mobile apps. Review and travel-reservation web sites are good examples. Not only may users want to access your offering on the go, but a mobile app can also be a great promotional vehicle. As users search and browse through app stores, it's just as important to be there as it is to be highly ranked in Google search results.

Today, having a mobile interface has become a competitive imperative, much like having a web site was a few years ago. Users comparing functionality

---

[3] www.nytimes.com/2011/03/07/business/media/07drill.html.

across products see mobile as a big gap if a competitor has an offering and you don't.

Getting a mobile application built may not be as challenging, time consuming, or expensive as you think. To get your iPhone or Android application built requires just three things. First, create a design for your application. Second, you need a set of application programming interfaces (APIs) to which the application can connect: for example, to upload files or download messages. Third, you need a developer or developers who can build the app. Online marketplaces like oDesk and vWorker.com make it possible to find developers who charge on a low-cost hourly or per-project basis.

Brand

Building a great brand is about being known for one thing. Lots of other web sites sold shoes, but online shoe retailer Zappos became known for its incredible customer service—people developed an emotional connection with the company and raved about it.

Your brand identity is critical as well—name, logo, icon, and even a single letter. *F* for Facebook. *P* for Pandora. Easiest and most powerful is to have the same company and product name. In a crowded world, there is little benefit in trying to market two brands—it's challenging enough to market one.

Things get exciting when you bring it all together. Delivered an order or a product? Ask your users to help spread the word by typing in a one-sentence description of why they loved your service and posting it to your web site and on their Facebook wall. That means more content for the search engines and more visibility for you, all driving more potential users to your site.

When one user invites another to use your application, support the integrated ability for both users to post that to their wall or tweet it. "I just started using..." might sound corny, and some users may opt out, but many participate. That drives up your visibility. Integrate the Facebook Like button directly into your product experience; don't just think of it as a piece of marketing.

Take a page out of today's social games. Reward your users with gifts such as free storage, discounts, and more, and then ask them to reciprocate by spreading the word about your product. Don't relegate ways for users to tell other potential users about your product to the marketing section of your web site. Instead, build those mechanisms directly into your product experience. At the time of upload, purchase, or in e-mails you send your users, give them quick and easy ways to share your product with the world.

Protect your brand. If you get a reputation for having a great product and treating customers and users well, you develop a great brand. Fail to fulfill your brand promise, however, and users will communicate that failure to others faster than you can tap out a tweet.

Summary

The seven ways to market your startup described in this chapter may seem overwhelming. It might appear that you have to be everywhere at once. But by engineering viral, mobile, and social capabilities into your product, you don't have to be—your marketing is an integrated part of your product, and vice versa.

What's more, with this approach and the marketing channels available today, you don't have to incinerate your hard-won cash to promote your company. By combining product investment that you need to make anyway with free and low-cost marketing mechanisms, you can achieve huge leverage on your marketing time and dollar investment. Through smart spending, testing, and iteration, you can then accelerate your marketing machine. Unsure how best to market your startup? Get help from someone who's been there and done it before.

Ultimately, great marketing means an incredible product combined with a clear, memorable message. What's so powerful about marketing today is that you can easily enlist your users in your success. To paraphrase Jerry Maguire, help your users help you.

To succeed, put the seven marketing approaches to work for you:

- Product innovation
- Viral marketing
- Social media
- Buzz
- Search
- Mobile
- Brand

Execution

Execution failure happens for all kinds of reasons—from failing to communicate effectively to never getting started, and from scaling too quickly to never scaling at all. Fortunately, you can avoid many kinds of execution failure.

If you've ever wondered how to communicate more effectively with your employees, customers, and investors, Chapter 7 holds the answers. Whether you're delivering good news or bad, choosing your words matters. And then of course there is that communication meeting that entrepreneurs spend hours both in and preparing for—the board meeting. You'll learn how to make board meetings productive for you, your team, and your board members. And you'll discover the most common communication failures that befall entrepreneurs, including failing to set expectations and not communicating at all—and how to avoid them.

In Chapter 8, I'll talk about one of the most common reasons potential entrepreneurs fail: they never get started. For those who have created multiple companies, starting a new venture may seem relatively straightforward. But if you've never quit your job, built a product, assembled a team, or raised capital, here's how—and why—you should start your company.

Time and again, companies fail as they try to scale because they don't focus. They don't attack their market effectively, they become complacent, they fail to hire to support growth, and they mismanage their cash. As you'll see in

Chapter 9, execution failures compound quickly in terms of time and cost. Once you have an organization in place, it's hard to change direction. Big organizations cost big money, and when you don't manage your capital properly, you can rapidly burn through tens of millions of dollars—and equity you can't recover—fast.

Great organizations can outrun the competition to become the market leaders, creating immense value for their founders, teams, and investors in the process. In Part III you'll come away with the knowledge you need to communicate your vision and your progress. You'll learn how to make the leap—and how to execute your way to scale once you do.

Failing to Communicate

Words Matter

Communication can make or break a startup. From board meetings to employees, from delivering good news to bad, communicating effectively can help make sure all the hard work pays off. Communicating ineffectively can infect an organization and waste incredible amounts of time and capital: developers build the wrong features while marketing prepares the wrong messages.

Bad communication often comes from failing to set expectations or not communicating at all. That can result in tough board meetings. Or, even worse, you can lose customers or users to the competition. People will forgive failure—but only if you communicate transparently with them about what's going on and right any wrongs. So why do so many leaders communicate so poorly, causing startups to fail, and how can you do it better?

Communicating Your Vision

Entrepreneurs are in the business of setting larger-than-life expectations. When you're creating something from nothing, you have to be. You have to wake up every morning believing in yourself and your vision—in the face of numerous potential investors, employees, and users all telling you that no, you're wrong. Your approach to the market won't work, your product won't work, your capital model is wrong, or they're just plain not interested in what you're doing. Up against all that negativity, entrepreneurs must continue to believe—and they must communicate that belief.

One of the biggest challenges entrepreneurs must address is balancing the day-to-day challenges of running the business while painting the picture of the big, transformative nature of their vision to investors, potential employees, and the public.

I recall one time when I was pitching my very first company to investors. It was the dark days of 2001, and not only were we on the road all the time talking to potential investors and customers, but when we were in the office, we were there until one or two in the morning and often later. Then we were back at it as soon as we woke up. To add even more stress, we were angel- and self-funded and had the fear of an impending empty bank account bearing down on us. An experienced investor who was a former entrepreneur met with us and listened to our pitch. He was, as they say, a serious guy, not one to mince words or use a lot of them.

I'll never forget what he told us. "You guys are back on your heels," he said. "I've been where you're at." We looked at him with raised eyebrows, skeptical. "You need to take a break, get some rest, and come back when you're fresh." It was the best piece of advice we had received in a very long time.

It also forced a very important issue. We were doing too much, and we couldn't do it all. We had to divide up our responsibilities and trust that they would get done; and we also needed to focus on what mattered. We couldn't continue to take meeting after meeting; we had to be more selective. As great as it was for relationship-building to meet someone in person, we had to start qualifying people first. And we had to narrow the scope of what we were building and get the core functionality right before we added more features.

Being frazzled meant that we weren't communicating well. We needed to refocus so that we could communicate our vision in a way that led to successful investment pitches and customer meetings. We stopped getting lost in the weeds when we were pitching because we weren't lost in the weeds in the day-to-day business.

It didn't mean we paid less attention to detail—if anything, we paid *more* attention. But by doing less, we were able to get more done, more successfully. And just as important, when we met with investors and customers, we focused on what mattered to them—not the minutiae of the day-to-day issues and details, critical as they were, that were very literally keeping us up at night.

Setting Expectations

Should you shoot for the stars and try to accomplish the seemingly impossible? Absolutely—that is what great startups are all about. That is your BHAG— your Big, Hairy, Audacious Goal. But never confuse your BHAG with what you need to accomplish day to day and the milestones you've promised to deliver on.

Identifying and communicating your BHAG and milestones separately makes everything easier and clearer: here's what we're shooting for, and here's where we are on the path to accomplishing that goal. That enables you to remain visionary while communicating actual progress and metrics.

To be an entrepreneur, you have to be somewhat irrational. The odds of failure are high. Yet the challenge of beating those odds, and the potential rewards, both personal and financial, are a big part of what makes entrepreneurship the calling that it is.

Hand in hand with that irrationality, however, go irrational expectations for yourself and your team. As a result, it's easy to fall into the trap of promising growth goals, such as revenue, profits, or users, which are wildly unrealistic.

The CEO of Company E was an incredible saleswoman. She had great success during the dot-com bubble, making hundreds of millions of dollars for her investors and herself. She was charismatic, and people were impressed with her from the moment they met her. She told investors what they wanted to hear: that her company was going to transform the industry by delivering a product that was 10 times more efficient than existing offerings. Not only that, but due to her relationships in the industry, she would be able to secure customer deals that others would only dream of. It seemed too good to be true—and it was.

Yet based on a combination of her past performance, her charisma, her relationships, and the vision she painted, investors flocked to her like moths to a candle. Having been through the fund-raising process many times before, she knew exactly how to manage it for an optimally priced capital raise. Once invested, investors became believers. They had to; after all, they had committed tens of millions of dollars to the endeavor, and to admit that the company was going to fail was to admit that they had made a very poor investment. With so many people saying it was a good investment, the company created a sort of frenzy, raising more and more capital, and making bigger and bigger promises. Of course, people from investors to employees had their doubts, but few wanted to question a CEO who could raise money so effectively and who seemingly carried so much weight in the industry.

CEO E didn't fail to set expectations. She overset them by miles. She lost track of the difference between her BHAG and the reality of where Company E's product and execution really were. In her mind, vision and reality became one and the same, and it was impossible, when she was communicating, to tell what was real and what was vision; the future and the present merged in her mind and in her communication. After spending more than $80 million in investor capital, CEO E's board replaced her, the company cut more than half of its staff, and the product remains a mirage.

CEO F, on the other hand, didn't overset expectations—he failed to communicate at all. After figuring out that his market was large but too early for his product, he withdrew behind his computer screen. Previously he had been a vice president at a large, public software company. He was used to things being a lot easier, and he was accustomed to pre-existing demand for a product.

As a vice president, his role was to iterate on a market-leading product that customers already wanted. Although managing a large team and working tirelessly to understand and prioritize new customer requirements was hard, it paled in comparison to the struggle he faced in finding product-market fit as head of his own company.

He faced a challenge he was unsure how to tackle, and he was too proud to admit that his original product-market thesis was incorrect. The struggle consumed him. He stopped communicating with the company and his management team. The last weeks of the quarter often found him on vacation. Meanwhile, he continued to promise unrealistic revenue and customer goals to his investors, even after his board gave him strong feedback to re-plan.[1]

Ultimately, faced with an unresponsive leader and still believing in the market opportunity, the board hired a Chief Operating Officer to run all of product, operations, and sales, leaving the founder as CEO in title only. Ironically, his board members were very successful entrepreneurs in their own right. Had he found the courage to ask them for help and had the willingness to receive it, they surely would have been happy to provide it.

---

[1] *Replanning* means revising an existing financial plan (often downward) based on new market or customer data.

Managing Board Meetings

If you've been a founder or executive at a company that's taken external financing, chances are you've been to a board meeting. Some people look on board meetings as a time suck—CEOs and their management teams spend days preparing for them and then sit through three or four agonizing hours of the meeting while board members often send and receive e-mails on their Blackberrys or iPads. Each month, these management teams look to the board calendar not as an opportunity but as a cost of having taken capital. There's a sentiment that's not all that uncommon: "If only my investors would leave me alone, I could actually get some work done."

A board meeting done right can be an opportunity not only to communicate important company information to the board—progress, challenges, key hires, financial metrics, and the like—but also to have real and valuable strategic discussions. It all comes back to expectations.

I don't have enough fingers and toes to count the number of founders and CEOs who have confided in me that they're worried about offending person X or a colleague of person X by calling that person out on something—their tardiness, their Blackberry use, or even a lack of expertise as it applies to the issues of the company. It's the founder or CEO's job to set expectations for board meetings, solicit input on what board members would like to have covered, and direct the meetings so they can be productive and efficient.

Toward that end, it's never too late for you to sit down with individual board members to communicate your expectations around the board meeting and understand what they would like to cover. Not having seen a board slide deck before isn't a problem—failing to ask for help is. Your board members and other CEOs are usually more than willing to share what has worked well and what hasn't.

Intimidated by the decades of experience some of your board members have? Don't be. Spending four hours accomplishing nothing is as much a waste of their time as it is yours.

Do board members consistently show up late? Talk to them offline, and then always start on time. Set a schedule for every meeting, and stick to it. Include specific times for breaks so people know there's one coming up and can plan their biological, e-mail, and telephone needs accordingly.

It may seem obvious, but make water and coffee readily available during the meeting, and provide snacks during the breaks. Staying focused during long meetings requires hydration and energy. Both are required to ensure the meeting keeps progressing. Avoid having a board meeting run through lunch if at all possible—the eating and noise will distract you and your board members. If you want to eat a meal with your board members, do so—just make it a separate event.

Send out board-meeting materials ahead of time so people have time to review them, and don't be shy about reminding them to review the materials before the meeting. Always include details like the start time, duration, and location of the meeting, and dial-in information even if no one has said they will be dialing in. Put simply, square away as many of the logistics as possible so you can make the time productive for yourself and everyone involved.

Tell your executives how much time they have, and get them to stick to it. Sloppy board meetings that start late and run late are often a sign of sloppy companies. Getting bogged down in an issue that clearly requires further discussion? Suggest a separate follow up. Is there a big issue on the table that no one is taking the initiative to discuss? Get it out of the way first; avoid letting the issue remain the elephant in the room and thereby causing the board meeting to fail.

Cover less material. Some CEOs feel it necessary to drill down in gory detail on every section. The reality is, it's not the job of your investors to critique the nitty-gritty details of your marketing programs, sales approach, or product features. They may have experience and opinions in some or all of those areas, but they invested in you because of the promise that you would innovate, manage, and lead.

Be your own toughest critic. Ask yourself the hard questions, instead of waiting for others to do so. If an area of your company is operating poorly, deal with the issue or hire someone to own it, rather than looking to your board to solve it for you.

Some CEOs shy away from giving details. By sticking purely to the big picture, they believe they can avoid being held accountable. Although this may be a strategy for raising money, it isn't a long-term strategy for success. Ultimately, many companies operated by these kinds of leaders suffer sudden and painful deaths or restarts.

In the case of Company B (a composite), the founder loved to talk about the product. He spent much of his time discussing the product, which was consistent with how he spent most of his time day to day. He did little else. Investors avoided confronting him about this but were a lot more interested in whether the product worked than in the details of how it worked. Unfortunately for the company, a lot of promises the founder made about what the product would do and how much revenue it would generate did not materialize. The product kept slipping as the company introduced ever-newer features.

No one wanted to be the bad guy. The founder was a temperamental individual who would surely hold a grudge. Moreover, none of the board members wanted to suffer the potential reputation cost of delivering bad news.

The investors had backed the entrepreneur and his vision, and they believed their only options were to fire him or give him more money. And the entrepreneur was very good at raising money, so there was a limited sense of urgency around forcing the discussion. The board members were worried that without the founder, other investors wouldn't back the company, employees would leave, and the company would be sold for pennies on the dollar.

The story didn't end well. A new investor, who believed in the market but had other ideas for the team, came in and recapitalized the company. The entrepreneur was offered an advisory position and remained on the board, but with no real input into product or strategy. Had the entrepreneur confronted the issues sooner, the story might have ended differently.

Delivering Bad News

Some founders—and even many experienced executives—shy away from delivering bad news. The best advice I ever received when being coached on how to communicate was, "Just say it." Not going to hit the numbers? Just say it. Hired someone who isn't going to work out? Just say it. But don't leave it there. Articulate your plan—what you're going to do about the issue.

What if you don't yet have a plan? Just say it. "We have this issue. We don't yet have a plan, but we're working on one, and we'd like to do a follow-up on—give your board members a specific date—to discuss the plan." It's a distant second to having a plan, but it demonstrates your leadership to your team and your board. Plus, the question is bound to be asked, so don't wait for it. Ask it yourself, and then answer it.

The other kind of bad news many people dislike giving is firing someone. I remember the very first person I ever had to fire. I agonized over it for weeks. How was I going to do it, and when? How would the team react?

Over and over again, founders have told me they've had the same experience: the team already knows that someone isn't working out and is waiting for you to take action. As much as you may agonize over letting someone go—perhaps that person was even introduced to you by an investor or a board member—your team is agonizing even more. Your team is working around that person, making up for issues, and expending effort to overcome a lack of chemistry.

It's one thing to talk about treating people with respect and another to do it. We've all read the cliché: firing someone—or getting fired—is really doing that person a service so they can go find what they're good at. There is some truth in that. But the key questions when delivering bad news are: Was it a surprise? Did you take action quickly? Did you deliver the news humanely? If the news came as a surprise—and it's critical to separate a person's emotional reaction to the news from the news itself—that is a failing on your part as a manager and leader. Again, it all comes back to setting and agreeing on clear expectations.

Delivering Good News

Suffice it to say that good news should be delivered far and wide. People like feeling appreciated, and when most people leave a job voluntarily it isn't because they were dissatisfied with their compensation but because they felt underappreciated.

Of course, great leaders set the bar high and have incredibly high expectations of their people. But they also communicate their appreciation when a team member goes above and beyond.

Recognition and appreciation are the most inexpensive yet most underutilized forms of compensation available. Don't give them out unless they're earned; but when they're merited, be generous with them.

Communicating with Your Team

One founder I know had to go away for two weeks due to a personal matter. He got back to discover that his small team of five engineers had all been hard at work—but on different features than they had talked about working on! When he asked them about this, each told him their version of what they thought they had agreed to work on. Of course, every developer had interpreted their work items through their own personal lens, interests, and sense of priorities.

An experienced executive shared with me a simple tactic he used for addressing a similar issue. He communicated key goals and then asked his team to write down the goals they had heard. He read what they had written down, they discussed it and had a good laugh about it (often what they had written was far different than what he said, or what he thought he said)—and then he communicated it again.

Team communication needs to be simple, clear, and frequent. It's not sufficient to follow the old rule: Tell 'em what you're going to tell 'em, tell 'em again, and then tell 'em what you told 'em. Communication can't be one-way—it has to be more interactive.

E-mail and social networks have revolutionized personal communication, making it much more frequent and interactive. When communicating with your business team, the same principles apply. As a result, the old rule, updated and adapted for startups, is as follows:

- Communicate your BHAG.
- Enlist your team in developing sub-goals and milestones.
- Communicate those goals to everyone clearly and concisely.
- Ask them what they heard.
- Repeat.

In other words: Tell 'em, ask 'em, repeat. Do more than tell—engage and interact.

Communicating with Customers

Communicating about events like new product releases is relatively easy. It's the crises that really test a startup.

At some point in its life, every startup faces a major product or customer failure. Intel, the chip manufacturer, faced such an issue in 1994 when a bug was discovered to be causing numerical calculation errors in its Pentium chip. The company initially decided to replace processors on the basis of need rather than request. Although the bug impacted very few people, the company was criticized for the way it handled the situation.

Legendary CEO Andy Grove later issued a full apology, saying that Intel's policy, "seemed arrogant and uncaring. We apologize. We were motivated by a belief that replacement is simply unnecessary for most people. We still feel that way, but we are changing our policy because we want there to be no doubt that we stand behind this product."

While it was late in coming, the Grove apology had a very positive impact on the company. Some marketing experts have even suggested that although the company had to take a short-term financial hit to reserve against possible product returns, the company's brand ultimately came out stronger than it began.

More recently, Airbnb, a web site that helps travelers find homes for rent, apologized publicly to a woman who rented out her home and then returned to find she had been robbed. Unlike the Intel blow-up, which took time to build, the Airbnb crisis came to a head virtually overnight.

Communication on the Web is near-instantaneous, and it means that once a negative story hits, it's all over the Web, all at once. People circulate stories in e-mail; they post, comment and tweet about them; and then they re-tweet and repost some more. That makes it more important than ever for startups to take the high ground and respond quickly when customer issues arise.

For Airbnb, the process was stressful for the company's management team and very painful for the woman whose home was robbed. It forced the company into action and produced a good outcome. The company created a new Trust and Safety Center and added an insurance policy for all those who rent out their homes.

Customer crises happen to every startup. In today's ultra-connected world, bad news spreads fast. Whatever the mistake, apologize to your customers and do it quickly. More often than not, you'll come out ahead.

Communicating Your Story

Some entrepreneurs are natural promoters. They have an inherent desire to be at the center of attention. Without delving too deeply into the psychology, the motivations are often simple: insecurity, narcissism, and/or a need for external affirmation. The result quite often is immense publicity for anything with which the entrepreneur is associated. Of course, when those same companies fail, the craters they leave behind tend to be big ones.

Other entrepreneurs are more inwardly focused and less promotional as a result. Some don't like the spotlight at all; others believe, as the old saying goes, that if you build a better mousetrap, the world will beat a path to your door. The reality is, promoters often have an easier time raising money, recruiting people to their cause, and getting user or customer adoption.

If you're not a natural promoter, hire someone who will work with you to get your story out, and commit to becoming a promoter yourself. Often the best promoters have a support staff behind the scenes booking them speaking engagements, getting them article placements, and helping them tweet and post.

Getting your story and point of view out is different than marketing your company's products. Communicating your point of view is about telling a much more personal story—it's about you and your vision of how you intend to do something transformational through the company you're building.

If you're three or four years in and you find yourself going along linearly, with no signs of increased growth, ask yourself if there's a way to reframe and position your story in a much more game-changing and human light. Become the go-to expert in your space. If you're intimidated or embarrassed by the thought of speaking at conferences, appearing on television, or being quoted, remind yourself of the upside: free marketing and publicity for your startup, which will create more customer demand, thereby reducing your chances of failure. And get some coaching; it may seem expensive if you're boot-strapped, but it will pay for itself many times over.

Summary

With the technology available today, communication is expected to be frequent and interactive.

Failure comes from

- Confusing your ultimate goal with your actual progress

- Mis-setting expectations

- Not apologizing for mistakes

- Poor management of communication logistics

- Failing to communicate interactively

- Not verifying that people heard what you said

To succeed:

- Separate your ultimate and short-term goals.
- Communicate frequently, especially during tough times.
- Set expectations.
- Apologize for mistakes, and make things right.
- Hold productive meetings with your board.
- Make communication interactive.

CHAPTER 8

Not Getting Started

How to Get Your Company Off the Ground

Many entrepreneurial dreams remain just that—thoughts on paper or in the mind of the would-be founder. And it's no surprise, because starting a company is among the most difficult and time-consuming tasks you'll ever undertake. But there are steps you can take to ease the mental burden and create the time you need to pursue your vision.

I spend so much time working with entrepreneurs on finding product-market fit, honing go-to-market strategies, and scaling their businesses that it's easy to forget that getting a startup off the ground can be equally daunting. I was reminded of this when an entrepreneur came to me with a compelling idea targeting a big market and then asked how she would go about getting started. For those of you who have already been through the team-recruiting and fundraising process, this may be old news. But for those who aspire to make the big leap and start their own business, this chapter should serve as a helpful guide on what to do—and what not to do.

Making the Leap

More startups fail due to people not taking the leap than for just about any other reason. Deciding to quit a steady job is hard, especially if you have a family, a mortgage, or other obligations. If you're not in or fresh out of college, one of the best ways to get a taste of what a startup is like is to join an existing one.

Big-company employees and executives often have the most difficult time adjusting to the reality of a startup.

Entrepreneur A always wanted to start his own company. He was often described by peers and managers as one of the most entrepreneurial people they had worked with. But something held him back. As a child, his family had struggled to make ends meet, and his parents had indoctrinated into him that getting a good-paying job at a large company was the way to go. After college, he immediately went to work for a big, established tech company where the salary was good but the upside was limited. He kept thinking about starting a company, but each time he almost made the leap, something prevented him: a tumble in the stock market, discouragement from his family about pursuing his dream, the pull of obligations and comfort of a steady salary, or the promise of promotion at work that he used as a justification to stay put.

Some years later, Entrepreneur A, now supporting a family and paying a mortgage, finally made the leap to start his own company after the big tech company where he had worked for so many years was reorganized. He agonized that he wouldn't be able to pay the bills and support his family, and yet this change had an incredible effect on him. He pursued his dream with absolute focus and the determination to make it a success. Not raising money, recruiting a team, and acquiring customers simply wasn't an option—he had to make his startup a success. As a result, he did.

There is nothing like self-motivation when starting a new venture. I wouldn't wish being broke on anyone, but from the perspective of someone starting a new company, if you're broke, you've got nothing to lose and infinite necessity. As a result, you're willing to take all the risk in the world. If you're rich, you can invest your own capital and probably convince other people with capital to put in money alongside you. Some investors will question your drive or ambition. The flip side to that, of course, is that having made some money, there's a good chance you want to make more.

Being neither rich nor poor may be the hardest starting point of all. A steady income and a comfortable lifestyle, combined with ongoing obligations, may make the prospect of ultra-high risk-taking daunting.

And then there is the prospect of a long period of time without work-life balance. People ask me about work-life balance and startups. They don't go together. There are jobs that can support work-life balance, such as lifestyle small businesses. But doing a startup isn't one of them.

I grew up working and helping to pay my family's bills. I shoveled snow in the winter, cleaned the school pool in the summer, and started writing software programs because it was a lot more fun and paid better than either of those other activities.

Even when I'm "not working," I'm working. Perhaps it runs in my family. My grandparents immigrated to the United States—they had no choice. When they got here, they were flat broke. Starting a business was their only option. They worked all the time to make ends meet and create a life for themselves and their family. Against the odds, all of their children went to college, and most of them went on to graduate school. Three of them became entrepreneurs in their own right.

Entrepreneurs are workaholics. They're obsessive about their products, users, and customers, and they work to fulfill that obsession. Those who are rich enough to retire build more products, start new ventures, and continue to try to change the world. Just look at Elon Musk, founder of PayPal, electric-car company Tesla Motors, and space exploration company SpaceX. Or consider Steve Jobs, founder of Apple, NeXT, and Pixar.

If this isn't your frame of mind—work as long as it takes and succeed at all costs—you should seriously reconsider launching a startup. You're likely to get part way into the endeavor and then fail for lack of desire to out-odd the odds.

But, that said, there is no better time to start a new company than right now. Dozens of people, when I asked why they decided to start something new, gave me the same straightforward answer regardless of age: "I realized if I didn't do it now, I'd never be able to do it."

Build a Big-Idea Company—Not a Company of Ideas

Before starting my first company, I spent a lot of time at Starbucks with my soon-to-be cofounders, brainstorming possible ideas. It was 2000, and although we knew mobile was going to be big, we weren't sure what we could build that would take advantage of the market trend. The devices of the time were archaic compared to today's smartphones, and we felt extremely limited by them as a result. We knew we wanted to build something on the device, but we weren't sure what.

Every month, and sometimes every week, we tried a new idea. In some sense, this was good, because it enabled us to test a lot of ideas quickly without getting overly invested in any one of them. We pitched our company at angel events and to various investors, but we didn't yet have *the big idea*—the catalyzing vision, articulated clearly and succinctly. We knew it, and they knew it.

As we were building our mobile web pages and applications for sending messages, however, we started to notice a trend. The pages weren't displaying consistently, and the messages weren't going through reliably. For a while, we were convinced the issue was our software.

To figure out what was going on, we built an automated service for sending and receiving text messages and checking the validity of mobile web pages. It turned out it wasn't our software that was the problem—it was the wireless networks and issues with the devices themselves. A lot of other people were experiencing the same issue and were willing to pay us for the monitoring and data our rudimentary service provided. Finally we were no longer a company of ideas, but a big-idea company. That project became the company, and the solution we built ultimately became Keynote Mobile Solutions.

Many people find coming up with new ideas for companies challenging. Faced with a blank sheet of paper, they realize they'd rather be iterating something that already exists. Coming up with the one right idea can be even more of a challenge.

Big ideas come from a founder's personal need to solve a problem, a wish to generate income, an overwhelming desire to transform a large market, or all three. Jeff Bezos is said to have written the business plan for Amazon.com on a cross-country drive to Seattle after worrying that he had missed out on the Internet gold rush. Pierre Omidyar created eBay after experiencing first-hand the inequalities of financial trading markets. Marc Pincus started gaming giant Zynga after playing video games and becoming frustrated that they weren't more social.

People have told me over the years that they would start a company if only they had a great idea. My response to them remains the same. Great ideas are right in front of you. If you don't have one, partner with a cofounder who has a great idea, or join an existing company. Many great operating executives would readily admit they're far better at scaling up companies than brainstorming new ideas from scratch.

A startup is a highly passion-driven and irrational endeavor. If you feel no passion for an idea or market, no overwhelming sense of desire to find a solution to a problem you're facing or to transform a market or the entire world, don't start a company.

Most company ideas are simply not big ideas. They're lifestyle businesses or small businesses. They can satisfy your personal lifestyle needs or generate an income, but they won't scale into big companies. The difference often comes down to goals and ambition: the desire to run your own scuba-diving school versus creating the leading dive school with franchises around the world; running a local bed-and-breakfast versus starting Hilton hotels; opening a local café versus creating Starbucks.

Big businesses start out as little businesses. The difference between those that scale and those that don't often depends on market opportunity and personal ambition.

If you're a technologist, perhaps you just want to build a piece of technology and flip it to Google or Facebook. That may be good for your bank account, but it won't result in a large company. It takes the same amount of work to build something big that it takes to build something small; the level of ambition, types of personal fulfillment, and skillsets required, however, are different.

What is clear is that although it's possible to start a company when you have lots of ideas, building a great company requires a single overarching idea: *the big idea*. Pierre Omidyar was working on multiple projects before eBay became *the* project. Marc Pincus started several other companies before finding his calling as an Internet entrepreneur.

Keep searching until you find *the big idea*.

Surviving a Lack of Capital

If you're trying to capitalize your new idea, and you're having trouble raising money, there are two possibilities. It's you or the investors. This can be a tough reality for the new entrepreneur to face.

When I started my first company, we invested our own savings and raised money from a few angel investors who knew us from our past jobs. It helped that we were incredibly naïve. Had we fully appreciated what we were getting into, it's likely we would never have left our comfortable jobs and started a company to begin with.

We pitched dozens of venture capitalists on that first company. At the time—late 2000 and early 2001—we also had no appreciation for financial markets and what these investors must have been experiencing as they watched their portfolios go from the highest highs of the bubble to the equally lowest lows of the bust.

The private markets, which include venture and angel investments in privately held companies, typically aren't as volatile as the public markets (such as NASDAQ and NYSE). However, the public markets and macroeconomic changes heavily influence private-market investors. These investors are influenced emotionally and psychologically as they watch their personal portfolios move up and down; they also take into consideration potential lack of downstream capital—that is, the ability of companies to raise more money later. If markets are down, that can reduce the ability of these private investors to make their companies liquid, get returns out, and raise additional capital. This leads to very specific "open" and "closed" windows when it's relatively easier or harder to raise venture capital or other sources of private financing for your company.

As a result, raising money isn't just about you and your idea—although that is certainly a big part of it. Raising money is about finding a match between you and your vision, and investors who not only buy into you and your vision but are capable of funding that vision as well.

Most new businesses aren't suitable for venture capital. And venture-capital firms can only invest in a relatively small number of new opportunities each year. Statistics indicate that of the millions of businesses created annually in the United States, fewer than 1,000 receive venture funding.

But there's more to it than that. Although most investors claim to be actively investing, many aren't. Timing may be bad. An investor may have just done a deal or a series of deals and as a result doesn't have the capital or bandwidth available to make another investment right away. Others are busy putting the capital and time they have into supporting their existing investments.

Investors who are part of partnerships may not have the ability to get a deal done—there may be partnership dynamics that prevent a particular partner from making an investment even if that partner wants to make one.

And some people who refer to themselves as investors may not really be what they claim to be! Before I knew much about raising money, I took it at face value that if someone was referred to us an investor, that's what they were.

It turned out that any number of funds and angel investors we pitched early on, before we knew what questions to ask and how to filter, were simply going through the motions—some people did it for social reasons, others did it because they were getting paid to look at new deals. When we raised money for our first company, a lot of the investors we talked with were in triage mode, trying to work their way out of the bust. Looking at a new deal—even without any intent to invest—may have been a welcome break from the reality of their portfolios.

There are dozens more reasons investors don't invest that have little or nothing to do with you. Some investors only invest in tech businesses; others only invest in non-tech businesses. Certain investors make only early-stage investments, whereas others make only late-stage investments. Investors may have minimum ownership requirements, amounts of capital they have to put to work, or return requirements to satisfy the expectations they set for their funds.

Others may already have a company in their portfolio that competes with yours. Conversely, some may be looking for a specific kind of investment—in a certain sector or at a particular stage—to fill out their portfolio. For example, a fund with a lot of earlier-stage investments might make a handful of late-stage investments to speed up the fund's time to liquidity (how quickly the fund can return money to its investors) to help with fundraising for future funds.[1]

And although it's easy to think of the investors you're talking with as the source of money, many investors—even some individuals—get their capital from other investors. Venture funds raise money from university endowments, large pensions, and *funds of funds*. Just as you make tradeoffs on how to spend your own money, institutional investors are constantly making tradeoffs on how to allocate their capital; these tradeoffs have little or nothing to do with your company.

Becoming disillusioned by repeated rejections is one of the shortest paths to failure. Keep in mind that numerous investors passed on Apple, eBay, Google, and Facebook, to name just a few well-known successes.

When I started investing, entrepreneurs would approach me about how they *needed* capital. As the old saying goes, the best time to raise money is when

---

[1] A venture capital firm typically consists of a managing entity/company that manages multiple funds. Funds are usually labeled sequentially, such as Fund I, Fund II, Fund III, and so on. Returning capital in one fund helps investors when they go out to raise money for a subsequent fund. Firms also create specialty funds targeted at specific technologies, sectors, or stages—such as seed or growth—to supplement the core funds.

you don't need it. Investors flock to you when your business is going gang-busters. Most run as quickly as possible in the other direction the minute they smell fear or desperation. This may seem counterintuitive—after all, Warren Buffet and others made their fortunes by finding companies that the market mispriced (that is, underpriced) and investing in them. But most people want to go with the flow, not against it. They want to join success, not create it.

Venture investors are by definition not value investors. Value investors look for fundamentals they understand combined with great-deal economics when they buy. In contrast, venture investors look primarily for companies that will grow quickly and become big, and that they can market to others once that happens.

Control Your Own Destiny

Keeping in mind that your business may not be suitable for particular investors, or investors may not be able to invest, it's still your job to finance your start-up. To do that, you have four non-exclusive options through which you can control your own destiny. And controlling your own destiny is critical to start-up success.

Rent and Ramen

The first option is to go on the "rent and ramen" plan. Cut your expenses down to the absolute minimum, and spend all your time validating the market need for your product. One way to do this is to create a few web pages and buy some ads to see if there is demand for your concept. Another way is to create mockups and show them to people. Or, you can build an ultra-simple version of your product and release a beta.

If you're not a developer, become one, or consider hiring some developers via an online development marketplace like oDesk or vWorker, programmers from a local university, or a friend of a friend. Of course, it would be ideal to build your product "right" from the get-go, but the reality is that you may have to plan on throwing that first version away and rebuilding it once you have enough capital to do so.

Nights and Weekends

A second option is the "nights and weekends" plan, where you keep your day job and fit your startup in around the edges. Although this plan is great in theory, in practice it's very difficult to make work. It can be useful for solidifying your idea, doing market research, or figuring out key unknowns, but it's hard to scale a business by building it nights and weekends.

Investors

A third option is to raise some money. Talk to angel investors, ask your friends, and pitch former colleagues. It helps if you've worked at a big tech company that has a bunch of wealthy current or former employees. Family members or others in your network can provide capital as well. Obviously, you can't go back and change your family history, but you can make use of every node in your network, every resource available to you. Getting into one of the well-known incubator or quick-start programs like Y Combinator or TechStars can be a great way to go. Put all these approaches together, and then make the funding last until you can raise more money.

Jeff Bezos was turned down by dozens of people, as was Scott Cook, founder of Intuit. If you've never raised money before—let alone asked people for money—the task can seem daunting.

Just remember, Girl Scout cookies are sold one box at a time, door to door. If the Girl Scouts can raise money for their cause, you can raise money for yours. Granted, the Girl Scouts have a great pitch, a great product, and a great brand. Make sure you have the same key ingredients.

Customer Financing

The fourth option, of course, is to build a profitable enterprise from the get-go by having your customers finance your company. If you know a customer, get a contract to fund the development of your product. Or, create something that generates revenue immediately.

While in business school, I spent a couple of hours in the library every day building web pages and buying traffic to send to those pages. Every time a user clicked an advertisement or filled out a lead form on one of my web pages, I made money. I started out making just a few dollars a day. Before I knew it, I was managing a team of outsourced ad buyers and had a $750,000 run-rate business on my hands, more than enough to pay for school.

Building the Team

Some days it may feel nearly impossible to pull a team together and even harder to keep one together once it's assembled.

Ideally, there are some people you've known for a while with whom you'd like to start a company, and whose skills are well matched to the company you want to start. Perhaps you knew them in your last job, in school, or through some other work connection. Regardless, you won't really know what they (and you) are like to work with as cofounders until you actually are cofounders. It's one thing to talk about starting a company and another altogether to work together day and night for months on end. Keep in mind, you're not looking for your whole team at once. You're looking for one or two cofounders with whom you want to work.

You can also go it alone. The common wisdom goes against this approach, but it has advantages. You set the direction and decide how to spend the money and what to do. Not a lot of meetings or disagreements—unless you like arguing with yourself, of course!

What about hiring? Your first few hires will be difficult. There is no way around it. In Silicon Valley, at least, talent is in demand, and people have the option of starting their own companies versus coming to work at yours. So it's paramount that you have something compelling, exciting, and game-changing to work on. Otherwise, there is no way for you to stand out from the crowd. Even the highest-profile, best-backed companies face challenges when it comes to hiring. Start with a great story, and work your network. Ask everyone you meet—lawyers, VCs, angel investors, and friends—if they know of great people looking to do a startup.

Users and Customers

Getting your first user or customer can seem like the hardest thing in the world. Some products lend themselves to early adoption by people you know. For example, if you worked in the storage industry and have been selling storage products, you probably can work your existing network and relationships. Or, if you're building, say, a consumer-facing mobile photo application, you can use the app yourself and tell your friends to try it. In both cases, you have a ready-made, easy-to-access user base.

The alternative is to try to get people you don't know to use your product. That can work—but it tends to be a lot more difficult.

If you're building a business application, call someone you know and ask them for some business, or advertise online. If you're building a consumer product, send invites to friends or generate scarcity, by, for example, creating the appearance of a limited number of available invitations. One way or another, you have to get the word out and test the waters.

You want visceral reactions. If people love the product, that is success. If people hate it, that is a form of success as well. Either way, you can take action on those reactions and avoid failure.

What you don't want is for people to be ho-hum about whatever you're doing—polite yeses will kill your company. You want to strike a nerve. You want whining and complaining. "If only it did this" is gold you can act on. "Seems interesting," however, is fool's gold.

Location, Location, Location

I founded my first three companies outside Silicon Valley. The San Francisco Bay area is prohibitively expensive, the competition is fierce, and talent is hard to come by. Yet there is no place like it. Successful, large tech companies have been built in other places—Microsoft, Amazon, and aQuantive in Seattle, for example—but the list is short.

The Bay area promotes a different level of risk taking and a very different view of failure than anywhere else. Starting a new venture or joining one is looked on positively even if the company ultimately fails. Experience with failure is an asset—you've learned on someone else's dime. Dozens of larger tech companies are looking to hire people with entrepreneurial experience to help them keep their organizations innovative.

The flip-side of the Bay area, however, is that loyalty is a lot harder to come by. People jump around more and are on the lookout for the next hot startup—which may be their own.

In the Bay area, practically everyone knows what "doing a startup" means. There is a lot you don't need to reinvent—legal paperwork and fundraising approaches, for example. You can spend your time focusing on your competitive advantage: that which differentiates you. You also gain the benefit of cofounders and employees who have started their own companies or worked at other startups.

The Bay area also has a very positive energy. Despite the vast number of startup failures, it has the bright outlook of constant reinvention that is infectious in its ability to help you succeed.

Of course, moving to the Bay area is not always an option or desirable. What's critical is to be able to recruit a team, acquire customers, and raise sufficient capital to build your company. It's easier to do that where there's already some startup infrastructure. If not Silicon Valley, consider a hub like New York City, which has a number of startups and early stage investors, or cities like Austin, Seattle, Boulder, Boston, or Chicago.

Summary

The biggest obstacle in the way of you starting a new company is you. To be an entrepreneur, you must be both idealistic and realistic. You have to believe the illusion that you'll succeed even in the face of hundreds of naysayers and statistics that indicate high odds of failure, while addressing the day-to-day realities of your business. This is what creates the emotional rollercoaster ride entrepreneurs so often talk about.

To avoid the failure of never getting started at all:

- Get started! There's no time like the present.

- Control your own destiny by controlling your sources of capital.

- Go out and get users or customers—get real-world feedback.

Failing to Execute

Lessons on Growth

One investor I know repeats the same refrain to every startup he works with: *focus wins*. The advice is as sound today as when he first gave it to me, along with a check, ten years ago. That's because without focus, it's impossible to lead, allocate resources, or define what winning means. Without focus, a company can't grow. Are your resources spread too thin? What do you do if you've lost focus? When should you hit the accelerator? How do the most successful companies execute at scale?

Lack of Execution

Listen to investors talk about a company that's not going the way they thought it would, and you hear one of two things. They either say the market isn't there, or they talk about execution failure. Statements such as, "Those guys couldn't execute their way out of a paper bag," "It's an A opportunity but a B team," and "We need to get someone in there who knows how to scale," are all too common.

If you've got a great market but you're failing to execute, admit you're wrong. It's not that great entrepreneurs don't make mistakes—they make tons of them. But they adjust quickly to correct them.

Sometimes execution failure occurs because people don't get along. There's no chemistry, people get on each other's nerves, they find they don't have enough common ground to make it work, or they can't agree on who's going to do what. They step on each other's toes. There is no easy solution to this kind of execution failure—the answer frequently is that someone stays and someone goes. But communicating about who's doing what—through both one-on-one meetings and weekly team meetings, not just casually—can help a lot. Success comes from tackling the big issues head on, not letting them linger.

Startups Are Fluid Organizations

Entrepreneur A interviewed more than a dozen candidates over the course of five months before deciding to hire one as his VP of sales. His board members, a number of them former operating executives, met with most of the candidates, some spending as much or more time with the candidates as Entrepreneur A himself. Yet the newly hired sales executive left the company after just three quarters.

The board and CEO conducted a post-mortem to try to understand what had happened. Three possible reasons were put forth:

- The company hadn't achieved product-market fit. Although there was some early traction with customers, even the most talented sales executive couldn't sell customers a product they didn't need.

- Although the VP of sales had been successful in previous jobs, he had been selling products that were very different than the one the company was building.

- Either the VP of sales didn't know how to build the kind of sales organization required to sell this product, or the right approach to selling the product hadn't yet been found.

One board member suggested organizational issues—that Entrepreneur A hadn't managed the VP of sales effectively and had, as a result, set up the VP of sales up to fail. As it happened, the VP of sales had run sales at one of the board member's other portfolio companies previously and had grown sales from $7 million to more than $50 million.

What really caused the VP of sales to fail will never be known for sure. Perhaps he was a decent sales executive but had lucked into a great opportunity at the previous company—a product that virtually sold itself. He put the right process and people in place, but the product filled such a critical market need that he didn't need to do all that much selling. Others argued that the VP of sales had implemented an innovative selling model at his previous company that caused the product to be successful.

Regardless of which factor caused the failure, what is certain is that it cost the company a lot of time and at least one additional round of funding. The VP of sales was in place for three quarters, and the search leading up to the hire took two quarters, counting the time the company spent deciding to start the search.

What's also clear is that no one—neither Entrepreneur A nor his board members—wanted to admit that something was very wrong. They preferred to let the illusion of "a little more time" deceive them, rather than face reality.

When it comes to human resources, startups must be incredibly fluid organizations. Although there may be some short-term public embarrassment when a high-profile executive leaves, the cost of keeping the wrong person in place or not figuring out the root cause of a company issue is far greater.

Startups by their very nature must be nimble and move quickly. It's one of the key advantages they have over their slow-moving, well-established, big-gorilla brethren.

As startups go through different phases, they need different people, and people with different skillsets and amounts of experience. Startups doing market discovery must optimize for trying a lot of things, failing quickly, and repeating until they find product-market fit. Startups that are scaling optimize for growth, and they frequently benefit from experience on the team in order to do that. That means the best startups are fluid organizations.

A startup should hire people who can address its immediate needs and its needs on a two-year time horizon. Some of those people will grow with the company and stay. Others will leave either because the startup doesn't progress the way they expect it to or because they find themselves unable to progress with it. In either case, startups that have static organizations fail. Those with fluid organizations succeed.

Under-Resourced or Over-Resourced?

It has been argued that a startup can never have too much cash. But surprising as it may seem, startups can fail both from over-resourcing and under-resourcing.

Startups spend the money they have. Teams that have too much cash early on don't force themselves to make the tough tradeoffs. They hedge their bets, fail to focus, and throw in features that aren't core to product success. They overhire and tend to spend too aggressively on acquisition, assuming they already have product-market fit or that they can solve problems through more aggressive sales and marketing, rather than a better product.

Startups that are under-resourced face the near-constant threat of going out of business or having to raise more money. Having bootstrapped multiple companies, I've experienced first-hand the agonizing decisions that have to be made when resources are scarce.

I remember several times when I wasn't sure we would make payroll—either because we were still negotiating a customer contract or because our funding had yet to close. Employees were depending on us to pay them so they could pay their bills—it was a heavy feeling of responsibility.

That lack of resources forced us to focus and make decisions quickly. Discussions about priorities became a lot easier. When it came to product features, we asked ourselves the following questions. If the answer was yes, we made including the feature a priority:

- Will this feature cause a customer to buy the product?

- Will not having this feature prevent a customer from giving us money?

- Will this feature help us acquire more users/customers?

We became brutally focused on product capabilities that would generate customers and revenue.

We found ourselves spending a lot more time thinking about user acquisition and how to create a great on-boarding experience. We agonized over the details of reducing friction between our product and our customers. We didn't want anything to stand in the way of someone using our product. And we devoted much more time to getting the word out, promoting our product, and figuring out new and innovative ways to market and sell. Ultimately, that focus on customer acquisition and revenue defined our company culture and approach.

Two incredibly successful entrepreneurs I know take this approach to an extreme. They're known for selling what they don't have. Given the choice between spending a dollar acquiring more users or a dollar on product, they spend on acquisition.

On the surface, they appear to be in grave violation of the mantra "under-promise and over-deliver." Products they're involved with take longer to build and have fewer features than promised. Yet when they do arrive, the products address very real market needs. What they lack in precision, they make up for in accuracy. These entrepreneurs know they can improve quality and add features as time goes on.

Because these entrepreneurs invest ruthlessly in customer over product, people question whether they're building companies for the long term. Their product teams often have to be overhauled with new heads of product and engineering. Yet they're masters at the product-market fit discovery phase so critical to startup success. Once they achieve product-market fit, they re-engineer their organizations and products.

Failing to Manage Cash

What's the main reason startups fail? It's axiomatic: They're undercapitalized. Or their burn rate is way too high. Or their financial recordkeeping is shoddy. Whatever the underlying reason, they go to write a check and find the bank account empty.

When it comes to spending, there is no single path to success. Some entrepreneurs swear by the "run at the wall, and the wall will move" strategy. This can and does work—but it tends to work best for venture-funded startups with multimillion-dollar checkbooks behind them. Conversely, any boot-strapped entrepreneur worth their salt has looked over the precipice of the zero-balance bank account and stared it down. It's easy to let yourself believe that investors are your only source of capital. They aren't. Customers can fund you, too. But the real question you must ask yourself is, "Why am I running out of capital?" The answer is where you started: product-market fit.

One of the biggest reasons companies run out of money is that they spend far too much before they're ready to scale. Until a company finds product-market fit, it's fine to run some low-cost user-acquisition experiments, but there is little point in spending huge amounts of money on acquisition.

Venture-backed entrepreneurs often assume that if they can't figure out their business with the current round of funding, they can get their current investors or new investors to invest more capital. They're exactly right until they're wrong.

Entrepreneur B had an unparalleled ability to raise money—investors loved his vision. Even when it costs tens of millions of dollars more than anticipated to fund his vision, he was able to raise the money. Investors overlooked the warnings signs that he was spending far too much while the economics of his market were changing. The prices of competitive products were coming down faster than he had anticipated, and it was taking him far longer than expected to get his product to market.

For a long time, investors disregarded this core issue, but eventually, after raising series D, E, and F rounds of funding, he met some investors who pushed hard on the crux of his business: would he be able to ship his product, and would it be at a price point that was competitive in the market?

Even though the existing investors wondered too, they held off on asking—because Entrepreneur B was such a great fundraiser. The conversations were short: "The guy just raised $50 million. How can we fire him?" But fire him they did, when he could no longer raise money.

The investors brought in an operational CEO who was the opposite of the entrepreneur. He replaced nearly the entire management team, got costs under control (that is, cut them almost in half), and restructured the company's debt. But the company had gone from being a rising star to a turnaround. Time will tell whether the turnaround is a success.

Bootstrapped entrepreneurs, conversely, have no one to rely on for capital but themselves, and potentially their angel investors, if they have them. I remember that when we bootstrapped our first company, we naturally went out of our way to save money. When we travelled, we looked for the best deals and stayed at the cheapest places we could find. We paid our bills on time, but we waited until they were due to send the money. We were frugal, and we negotiated hard.

I credit our upbringing for that—we all came from families where money was treated with respect. We were raised to make money and save money. As a result, it wasn't hard to act similarly when we started our company. But we did face some significant challenges. Being bootstrapped meant we were constrained. Once we had paying customers, we couldn't keep up with their demands because we were constantly making tradeoffs on what to build. But that also meant we were extremely focused.

If you're venture-backed, it's easy to get sucked into the false security of having what is, by any measure, a lot of money in the bank. The problem is that the more money they have, the more companies spend. Salaries go up, costs go up, and people become less frugal. Managed properly, these companies can potentially grow much faster, leading to greater successes—or bigger craters.

Debt

Debt can compound cash mismanagement. Some venture investors characterize debt for startups as "the banks loaning us our own money." This is because debt for startups often isn't backed up by receivables or revenue, but by the venture investors and the capital they've invested.

In my corporate finance class at the Stanford Graduate School of Business, a legendary finance professor once opened a door on the stage of the auditorium in which he was teaching.

"Do you hear that?" he asked us. All we heard was silence. We looked at him like he was crazy. He slammed the door shut. The room went from silent to deathly silent.

"That's the sound of the debt monster." Debt can provide great leverage on existing capital to accelerate a business. It can also devour a business as quickly as our professor slammed that door shut. For early-stage startups, debt can seem wonderful when things are going well. But when they aren't, the company still has to make payments. Even as you're producing revenue, a chunk of that revenue goes to pay off your debt every month. Even though you're working hard, debt can drown you.

Entrepreneur C nearly drowned not because of debt but because of his lease. Long-term leases have proved very difficult to get out of. It's possible to sublet space, but doing so typically requires approval of the landlord. And if you're already subletting, you have multiple levels of approval to contend with. Entrepreneur C signed a long-term lease for a lot of space at the height of the Internet bubble.

When the bubble crashed, the loss of numerous customers was compounded by the large amount his company had to pay every month for its lease. No matter how hard the company tried, it was impossible to break even because the lease payments were so high. It took the company years to become profitable.

When you have a lot of cash, problems seem small, right up until there's not a lot of cash—and then they seem really, really big. Failing to manage cash, whether it's a lot or a little, is one sure way to make your company fail.

Cash Flows from Product-Market Fit

You can't fake product-market fit. Sometimes you can use vast amounts of capital to cover up core business problems. But in the end, you must achieve a match between a great product, a big market, and the ability to reach that market *efficiently*. Ultimately, the truth will out, and you have to build something people want. Otherwise, you'll run out of cash.

Many execution reasons can cause you to run out of cash—cash mismanagement, bad collections (customers who don't pay), fraud, theft, ignoring problems, and not watching the numbers. Getting these elements of a startup right requires experience and skill, and you can often hire to manage them.

Product-market fit requires deep knowledge of your domain. That can be your own needs if you're building a consumer product for yourself. Or it can be deep knowledge of a customer or market need if you're building something for others. Either way, you can't hire to find product-market fit—you must find it yourself.

Executing Early vs. Executing at Scale

During the product-market fit discovery process, you should expect to get a lot of things wrong, as long as you get the product-market fit discovery process right. If you don't bring the discovery process to a successful conclusion, the rest of the items don't matter.

Perfection is your enemy when you're executing early. Get your product out fast, and ask for feedback. Get some money in the bank, even if it's not on your ideal terms or the exact amount you wanted to raise. Be flexible about everything—but don't compromise on finding product-market fit.

Finding product-market fit requires either being right out of the gate—possible but rare—or trying a lot of different things and failing at them quickly until you discover what works.

In contrast, executing at scale means optimizing for growth. Instead of trying many different things, growth-stage companies attempt to replicate what's working. Entrepreneurs who are great at the product-market fit discovery process may or may not be great at scaling up.

Some entrepreneurs fail at this transition because they stop focusing on delivering great products. Other entrepreneurs focus on product to the exclusion of all other company functions: they're unable, in particular, to hire people to manage functions like finance, sales, and human resources.

One entrepreneur I know is amazingly detail-oriented. This level of detail extends to all areas of his life. Even though his personal net worth is in the tens of millions of dollars, he still does his own taxes. He excels at operational detail.

Conversely, speed isn't his strong suit. When he first became an entrepreneur, he struggled with this conflict. After many years, however, he learned to hire to backfill his weaknesses. He spends his time focused primarily on technical and process aspects of his business that require intense rigor and attention to detail.

Many creative entrepreneurs find the process of scaling up tedious and boring. Or scaling up is so foreign that they stop trusting their instincts. One solution to this problem, articulated by serial entrepreneur Niel Robertson, is to look for hires from companies that are 12–36 months ahead of where you are. Don't hire for the needs of your business today; instead, hire for where you need to be 24 months from now.

Also consider hiring from companies that are ten times bigger than yours. If you hire people from organizations much, much larger than yours—say, 100 times bigger or more—you run the risk they'll be too "big company" for your startup. And if you hire people from companies that match where yours is today, you risk outgrowing them quickly. You want to gain the benefit of experience but not have that experience be more than two years out. The key is hiring at the middle of that experience curve.

Hiring Help to Scale

A famous venture capitalist once reportedly said, "I never fired a CEO too soon." Although this may be the classic wisdom, another famous investor said, "[Running the company] is the founder's job to lose." In other words, investors shouldn't back founders who they don't think can lead their own companies, and founders shouldn't start companies they don't think they can lead. It's the founder's job to run the company until they prove they can't do it.

How do you choose a great founding team? What works and what doesn't? How do you know when you're not scaling as fast as your company—and what do you do about it? Should you ever fire yourself?

It's rare to find an entrepreneur who is both a great product visionary and a fantastic operator. By definition, product visionaries see how their product and the world should be; great operators are pragmatists who see the world primarily as it is. A few rare people are able to work at both ends of the visionary/operator spectrum simultaneously, or at least easily switch between them.

But many of the most successful tech companies have separate people in these roles. Mark Zuckerberg is the product visionary at Facebook; Sheryl Sandberg is the operator. Larry Page and Sergei Brin were the product visionaries at Google while Eric Schmidt, until recently, was the operator. Bill Gates had Steve Ballmer, and Steve Jobs had Tim Cook.

What worked so well with these partnerships was that the founders maintained their roles within the company—setting product direction—while the operators managed the operations. Yet sometimes this simply isn't possible.

Entrepreneur D was a big fan of hiring a COO. Inexperienced at operations but a world-class product visionary and promoter, he raised tens of millions in venture capital and scaled his business quickly. But the details of finance, sales, and legal issues frustrated him. His board members suggested that he hire a COO, and he agreed. Yet he faced numerous challenges in making the hire.

Entrepreneur D mostly delegated the hiring process to his board members—not because they asked him to but because he didn't want to deal with it. The board spent several months interviewing candidates, and the same thing happened on each potential hire: the candidate talked politely with the board members but wanted to talk with Entrepreneur D to understand what he was like to work with.

The entrepreneur, who kept himself extremely busy, didn't make time to meet with the candidates. Weeks passed between the initial meeting with a board member and the follow-up meeting with Entrepreneur D—and then he would often cut the meeting short because he had other meetings to go to that he felt were equally, if not more, important. Candidates came away with the impression that Entrepreneur D wasn't interested in hiring them. They were right—he wasn't.

Entrepreneur D faced another challenge. His standards were high—a great thing. But he had a vision of what his ideal COO was like, and each time he met someone, he found several things wrong with the candidate. Although some of the people he interviewed went on to become successful COOs at other high-profile startups, none of them matched his requirements on all dimensions—none of them were perfect.

The final challenge Entrepreneur D faced was that of the few candidates whose failings he could look past, none wanted to work for him. The truth was that even though Entrepreneur D recognized he wasn't properly managing the operational aspects of his business, he didn't want to give up the control that bringing in a COO entailed; and he didn't really want a partner in the business, even though that partner would be operationally focused while Entrepreneur D would continue to be the external face of the company and drive all product direction.

One board member only half-joked that Entrepreneur D liked the operations of the company being slightly sloppy and remaining as they were when the company was smaller, because even though the company wasn't operating optimally, it allowed the entrepreneur to maintain complete control. In fact, because Entrepreneur D's board members had no way of fully knowing what was going on inside the company, they had little choice but to go along for the ride—or fire Entrepreneur D.

After a year of conducting the COO search, that is exactly what they did. It wasn't smooth, and the company lost its product visionary—and its way. Later, it came out that numerous business-development deals the company had entered into jeopardized the core of the company's business. Only after two years and an additional round of funding did the company find its legs again and get back on track. Whether it will be a success is yet to be determined.

Entrepreneur E faced a different problem. He hired a COO quickly, but the COO turned out to be a terrible hire for the company. Although the COO acted knowledgeable and had a great resume, he wasn't very good at his job. Put another way, he "talked the talk" but didn't "walk the walk."

The company could have avoided this problem by taking more time to meet with multiple candidates. Although the company desperately needed an experienced executive to help it scale, Entrepreneur E rushed into the hire and regretted the result. "If we don't get someone in here quickly, it'll cost us," is a difficult statement to disagree with. But the counterargument holds more weight: getting the wrong person costs more.

As one investor I know is fond of saying, if a company that's in a great market with a great product that's selling is struggling, the answer is almost always "hire." If you're a product visionary, team up with a great operator. It's rare that this happens at the founding stage of a company, because great operators need something on which to operate! They also tend to operate at scale—in the growth phase of a business—not in the product-market fit discovery phase. If you're a great operator, find an incredible product visionary. And if you think you're both, ask yourself how you can have the biggest, most highly leveraged impact on your business. Then hire an all-star management team to handle operational functions such as customer service, sales, finance, marketing, and legal.

Know Your Numbers

As the Cheshire Cat said in *Alice in Wonderland*, "If you don't know where you're going, any road will get you there." If you don't know your numbers, it's very hard to predict when you'll need more capital and which of your activities is having an impact on your business. How can you know where to invest if you can't measure what's working and what's not?

One CEO I know always hesitates slightly before he talks about the "cash out" date of his company—that is, the date his operating plan indicates his company will run out of money, not the day he gets to cash out his stock for millions of dollars. He views any discussion of running out of money as a negative. He used to put this number at the very end of his board-meeting presentations. One day I suggested he put all the numbers up front. Just put it all out there—the good, the bad, and the ugly. He asked me, "Won't my investors find that disturbing?"

"I doubt it," I told him. After all, for angel and venture investors, most of their companies are always running out of money! The time a company has the most money is the millisecond after a new round of funding closes. After that, the company's cash balance gets lower and lower right up until more funding closes or the company becomes profitable. During portfolio reviews, investors spend a lot of time on capital planning, cash positions, and the future cash needs of companies. That's because understanding and managing the capital needs of their portfolio companies is a big part of an investor's responsibilities.

Board members find it disturbing when CEOs miss their numbers when they're supposedly in the scale-up stage of their business. But they find it *really* disturbing when CEOs don't present critical information up front—or at all.

Waiting makes people think you're hiding something, reduces your credibility as a leader, and takes focus away from the most important challenges a business faces. Changes and unexpected events are to be *expected* at a startup.

Knowing your numbers is critical to operating your business:

- What is the slope of the growth of your business? That is, how fast is your business scaling?

- Which activities and features result in customers or users sticking around?

- Which areas of marketing activity and spending produce the most results?

- How much is a user worth to you?

- How much money are you burning every month?

- If you had more money, what would you spend it on? In other words, is what you're doing to acquire users and customers repeatable, and just a question of capital and people constraints?

As it happens, these are the very same questions investors will ask you when you go to raise money.

The Goal: Repeatable, Profitable Acquisition

Knowing your numbers tells you whether you've built a repeatable, profitable acquisition mechanism. You know how much it costs to acquire and serve a user or customer, and how much that user is worth to you, during the lifetime they're a user of your product. Everything in a scaled-up organization is in support of building a great product and then feeding and optimizing the machine that attracts, retains, and monetizes the users of that product.

If you try to create the machine before you have product-market fit, you waste a lot of time and capital. That's why, according to the *Startup Genome Project*, the number-one cause of startup failure is premature scaling. Premature scaling means spending money too quickly, which causes startups to run out of money before they have a chance to iterate their way to product-market fit. It also means startups that suffer from premature scaling lose the nimble approach that is core to being a startup. They've overcommitted to an organization and approach before they know what organization and approach they really need.

Although business schools teach over and over the importance of treating *sunk costs*—money that is already spent—as irrelevant to future investment decisions, the reality is that sunk costs play a strong psychological role in both investor and entrepreneur decision making. By scaling prematurely, not only do you have a physical organization and associated high burn rate in place, but you also have a larger psychological hurdle to overcome if you want to change direction. Early-stage startups that haven't yet found product-market fit are all about preserving optionality. Startups that have entered the growth phase are primarily about optimizing for scale while introducing relevant features and updates to keep the core product attractive and competitive.

The Myth of First-Mover Advantage

Investors are fond of talking about *first-mover advantage*, which is the apparent advantage gained by the first entrant in a new market. Some first-movers are able to capture the market and create monopoly or near-monopoly-like businesses.

Many of today's market leaders, however, didn't have first-mover advantage. Facebook wasn't the first social network, the Apple iPod wasn't the first portable digital music player, and Google didn't create the first search engine.

Quite often, pioneers end up with arrows in their backs, while one of the later movers learns from the pioneers, executes better, and takes the market-leadership position.

Numerous entrepreneurs and CEOs have claimed that their companies were "a little too early" for the market. Investors just needed to be patient. Yet even having admitted that the market didn't exist or that they hadn't figured out a way to reach the market, they chose not to cut their burn rates to match their scaled-back revenues, switch go-to-market strategies, or change markets.

Many of them were too heavily invested in their existing plans, were convinced it was a matter of executing better than they had been, or put ego ahead of reality. As a result, they ran out of money and failed.

These companies didn't cut back their burn rates, so they needed more capital. They couldn't raise that capital not because they lacked vision or execution—

many of them had both. Rather, they took too long to match vision to reality. Investors will suspend disbelief for some period of time. But ultimately, they'd rather put their money into companies that are growing than ones that aren't.

How the Late Entrants Won

How did Facebook beat early market leaders MySpace and Friendster? How did Apple beat the existing digital music players? How did Google beat the other players in search, including Excite, which started long before, in 1993?

Unlike its competitors, Friendster and MySpace, which focused on helping people meet new people, Facebook focused on keeping people connected with those they already knew. People feel more comfortable connecting on a social network with those they already know than with people they don't,[1] and that that was a much bigger need than meeting new people.

In terms of its go-to-market strategy, Facebook started with a niche—universities—and used that to make real identities and authenticity a core value, whereas profiles on MySpace and Friendster were much more likely to be exaggerated or made up. Although anyone can now join Facebook, Facebook originally gave the site exclusivity by limiting who could join. That drove demand for the site.

Facebook did nearly everything a startup is supposed to do right: it was nimble, reacted quickly, and got the product right. In contrast, its biggest competitor, MySpace, was mismanaged as part of the larger organization of News Corp. Describing its handling of MySpace, News Corp. CEO Rupert Murdoch said, "We ... proceeded to mismanage it in every possible way."[2]

Google won because the company focused on search to the exclusion of all else. By implementing a new approach to generating search results based on the relationships between web sites, Google delivered more relevant results than any other search engine.

Even Google's closest competitor, Yahoo!, switched from serving its own search results to using Google's. And as the number of web sites and pages

---

[1] *How Facebook Won the Battle of the Social Networks*, Innosight, November 16, 2010. www.innosight.com/blog/564-how-facebook-won-the-battle-of-the-social-networks.html.

[2] *The Guardian*, October 21, 2011. www.guardian.co.uk/media/blog/2011/oct/21/news-corporation-annual-meeting-live#block-33.

Google indexed grew exponentially, it continued to deliver a better product experience, driving down the time required to deliver search results.

Although other companies developed MP3 players before Apple, Apple was the first to get the end-to-end consumer experience right, from the design of the device to the software for loading music. And like Google and Facebook, Apple won by selling benefits—a better experience—not features.

Apple coupled the sleek iPod device with an equally sleek marketing campaign. The iPod was easily recognizable, from the device to the white earplugs. Apple and the iPod became a statement, not just a functional device.

Become the Market Leader

What if you're not the market leader? It's the elephant in the board room, the difficult question no one really wants to ask: "We're #2. How do we become #1?" If you don't answer the question, #1 will answer it for you.

The advantages of market leadership are obvious. Investors (private and, later, public) want in and are willing to pay for the privilege. As a result, market leaders can raise more capital on better terms than any other player.

They have pricing power. Because they're #1, customers and users want to go with them, so they can charge a premium. And their brands are the best known, so user and customer acquisition costs are lower.

Becoming the leader may seem like a daunting task, but there are some proven ways to succeed:

1. *Decide to win:* Deciding you want to be #1 is probably the most important part of becoming #1. If you're comfortable at your company and things seem to be going okay, you'll never become #1.

2. *Build great product:* As you've seen with the examples of late-market entrants, focusing on the right product and the right way to deliver that product to market can enable you to beat out the other players.

3. *Move faster than the market:* Many startups give up the agility that is a startup's inherent advantage in favor of overly long-term planning and slow execution. They take too long to hire, agonize over strategy changes, and reduce their appetite for risk, nervous about how investors will respond to radical changes.

    Yet risk-taking, innovative approaches, and moving quickly are what make startups succeed. If you've settled into a comfortable existence at your startup, shake it up so you can move faster than the market.

4. *Shatter the myth:* In some cases, #1 by all measurable accounts (revenue, market position, number of users, or capital raised) is #1. But in less-developed markets, it's often more marketing than reality. Don't be "all steak no sizzle" and let yourself get outmaneuvered by companies that have great marketing but less-worthy products.

    Up your profile, get visible, and market like crazy. Every time #1 is mentioned, you want to be mentioned. Shatter the myth through marketing, PR, and customer acquisition. Implement a partner strategy to make yourself bigger than you are alone. Make your reality the market perception.

5. *Make being #2 an asset—until you're #1:* This is the Avis "We Try Harder" strategy. Organizations with existing products simply can't move as quickly. They have to consider their existing user, product, and cost investments when making changes. This is the quintessential startup strategy: be more nimble than #1.

    Some companies take a *fast follower* strategy as the #2 players in a market. They copy many of the product and go-to-market strategies of the #1 player, and then, if #1 stumbles, they leapfrog ahead.

6. *Make it easy to switch:* A trail first blazed by Excel/Notes and Word/Wordperfect, these products made it easy to switch by implementing the same keyboard short-cuts as existing products. With little to no behavior change, users were able to do everything they'd always been able to do and take advantage of a host of new features as well.

    More recently, this has happened in the form of e-mail and contact importers, which make it nearly friction-free for users to take their contacts with them. Fea-tures like importers and migration tools may seem un-glamorous to build, but they're pivotal in getting users to switch.

7. *Be open when others are closed, and closed when others are open:* This is the strategy Google took with Android (open) in the face of Apple (closed). Google, with An-droid, gave the other players in the market (that is, the other phone manufacturers and wireless carriers) a via-ble alternative to the Apple iPhone. This works excep-tionally well in markets where the existing ecosystem feels threatened.

8. *Roll up the market:* With the right capitalization strategy, you can go on the offensive, acquire some subset of the #3 through #10 players (by market share), and become #1. Vacation-rentals site HomeAway (which went pub-lic in June, 2011) applied this approach very success-fully—it rolled up a market of smaller players to be-come the big kahuna.

    Proper investor backing and valuation are critical to this strategy, along with an organization that can execute on it. When executed well, acquiring your next-largest competitor is a time-proven way to accelerate cus-tomer adoption, revenue, and growth. Just make sure your organization doesn't die of indigestion.

9. *Use white-space innovation:* Some companies are so caught in their legacy businesses or existing approaches to the market that they find themselves unable to avoid a decline into oblivion. Most people think this only happens in big companies, but it happens to startups that have been around for a while as well.

   A product has been selling, but relatively slowly. The startup may be profitable, but it's the law of small numbers—the company stays in business but has reached a local maximum, and rapid growth seems near impossible. The company exists in the shadow of much larger players that are dominating its market or an adjacent market.

   Taking a white-space approach can free a company to go from laggard to leader. It requires a team that is empowered to build the best product, free from the legacy obligations of the existing business, and not held hostage by the existing organization.

10. *Pour on the gas once you have product-market fit:* When you have product-market fit, you know it—you can feel it. Things are on fire. Users are signing up in droves. Sales people aren't just saying things like, "This product sells itself!" they really mean it. It's time to scale up. Focus on organizational growth combined with ramping user growth, for consumer companies, or customer growth, for business companies—as fast as you possibly can.

When the Market Outruns You

Startup founders often find they're too early to a market or that their product isn't a fit for what the market wants. Sometimes, however, the market outruns you.

Later entrants can enter a market in which you were an early player, quickly understand the core features that users or customers want, and focus on those. They aren't weighed down by the baggage of trying lots of different approaches—instead, they can see what works and perfect just that.

Entrepreneur X set the vision for his startup based on trying to address his own needs as an executive at a large company. An ahead-of-his-time thinker, when he developed his product, it addressed his needs but was so far ahead of what the market was ready for that adoption was very slow.

However, Entrepreneur X was an evangelist. He educated the industry on the need for his approach. Meanwhile, in an attempt to get customer adoption, Entrepreneur X's team added more features and changed the company's product focus. Entrepreneur X kept promoting his vision, but his product no longer matched that vision.

Competitor Y entered the market two years later. The company focused on the core functionality Entrepreneur X had promised and delivered a very compelling, easy-to-use product. Other entrepreneurs, seeing the success Competitor Y was having, entered the market as well.

Practically overnight, a market that had been moving slowly erupted with a frenzy of activity. The market became crowded with products and noisy with marketing messages. Company Y stayed focused, whereas Entrepreneur X's company spent months pivoting back to its original plan. Of course, by the time his company did that, it was game over—Competitor Y had a huge lead in customers, revenue, and mindshare.

Coming from behind after another company has passed you is very difficult. You need the leader to stumble or become complacent, you need a must-have innovation that leapfrogs the leader, or both. There is incredible momentum in being the leader; that momentum is difficult to regain once you lose it.

It can be done, however. Apple regained its momentum, but it took the return of its founder, years, and a new product line to do it. IBM regained much of its momentum, but it took a new CEO—Lou Gerstner—a new strategy, and a shift in culture. GE got its mojo back, but it required a new CEO—Jack Welch—who implemented radical restructuring and the "Be #1 or #2" mandate.

Regaining market leadership, unlike getting it in the first place, is a turnaround situation. Turnarounds, by definition, are difficult. And although they might seem toughest for large organizations, they're doubly hard for small ones. When big companies are on the verge of going out of business, a lot of people and institutions have a vested interest—customers, investors, shareholders, suppliers, employees, even the government. When small companies are on the verge of going out of business, a few people care deeply, but the vast majority do not. You must save yourself.

Your options are as follows:

- *Bring in a new leader:* Although it may seem unlikely that a new leader would want the job, there is a set of people who enjoy the unique challenges of a turnaround. Investors are often willing to provide more capital behind a new leader. Like organ transplants, new-leader transplants can face a host of complications, including rejection. An experienced investor once told me that bringing in a new CEO is a 50/50 proposition at best. But sometimes an injection of new leadership—regardless of the leader—is what a company needs to regain its footing.

- *Sell the company:* Of course it's better to sell when you don't need to than when you do. But this must be considered as an option.

- *Focus, focus, focus!* Companies that need to regain a market-leadership position have often lost their way and lost their focus. They have too many products, they lack a clear vision, and they struggle due to poor execution. The advice I was given by an investor ten years ago is as applicable to turnarounds as it is to new investments. Focus wins.

Summary

Great execution can't deliver product-market fit, but a lack of great execution can kill a company that has found product-market fit.

When it comes to execution, one of the biggest challenges entrepreneurs face is organizational—hiring for growth.

Startups that have been around for a while and that haven't hit the growth curve they desire are often hesitant to shake things up due to the emotional and psychological investment in sunk cost. To succeed, leaders of stagnant startups must fight the siren song of sunk cost, while leaders of high-growth companies must scale their organizations to support the growth.

Market leaders have proven time and again to deliver the most value for investors and entrepreneurs alike. Great product-market fit combined with unparalleled execution will move a company from market laggard to market leader.

Capital and Liquidity

Startups live and die by whether they have enough money in the bank. In this part of *Why Startups Fail*, you'll earn about a different kind of product-market fit: when *you* are the product and investors are the market; and when your company is the product and larger companies interested in buying yours are the market.

Whether you're looking for an angel round of funding, or raising tens or hundreds of millions, *how* you pitch can have just as big an impact as what you're pitching. In Chapter 10 we'll explore the motivations that drive investors: greed and fear. I'll talk about the key reasons so many pitches fail—and how to avoid them. You'll come away equipped with the ability to frame properly and connect with your audience. And you'll understand that all-to-obscure entity, the investment partnership, and how to put it to work for you.

Having built their companies for years, far too many entrepreneurs leave money on the table when it comes time for a "liquidity event"—selling or merging the business. They get outmaneuvered by experienced investors or corporate development teams. In Chapter 11, you'll learn how to get paid for your work. Many potential merger and acquisition transactions (which account for some 90 percent of liquidity events) that seem promising at the outset end up failing. You'll learn the common reasons why and how to avoid them—starting with planning long before your company approaches a liquidity event.

In Chapter 12, we'll see how *focus* combined with *failing fast* leads to success. I'll cover some of the rewards and tradeoffs involved in doing a startup— including the myth of working for yourself. It has been said that success has many parents while failure has few. I'll conclude with a summary of the key reasons for startup failure and how you can learn from them to make your startup a success.

Pitches That Fail

Perfect Your Pitch

Many an entrepreneurial dream has failed because the founder got in front of the right people with access to capital but failed to woo the audience successfully. This chapter is about how to succeed when pitching your idea.

There is no perfect pitch. When I was raising money, every investor responded to something slightly different. Ultimately, nothing speaks louder than a big market, a disruptive product, and an incredible team. But a great pitch can really help you tell your story. And telling your story well is just as critical in getting potential employees to come work for you as it is in raising money and getting users. What has caused entrepreneurs to fail in raising money? Why do some entrepreneurs raise millions while others can't attract any outside capital at all? How and when should you pitch? How can you transform your pitching approach?

Pitch the Right Investors

One major reason pitches fail is that entrepreneurs pitch the wrong investors. Most startups, even technology startups, aren't good candidates for venture capital. And as I've discussed previously, there are many reasons an investor may not invest—timing may be off, investors may be short on funds or looking for specific kinds of investments, or they may just be bad at picking good deals. Many investors passed on great opportunities like Apple, Google, Facebook, and others, to name just a few.

Conversely, some investors will be deeply knowledgeable about your market or approach because of previous experience in the space or a strong belief or investment thesis about a particular market opportunity. These investors are ideal—you don't have to convince them of the opportunity, only that you're the likely winner in the space. By any measure that is still a tall order, but it's a much easier one to get.

Some investors are momentum investors—they invest primarily in companies they believe are already rising stars. Others are marquee investors—they want to invest in people who are big names or who come from large, well-known companies. Certain investors prefer to invest only in people they know.

Before you pitch, figure out who you're pitching and what their style is. How can you find out if an investor likes a space and what their investment thesis is? Ask! Look at their portfolios. Talk to the founders of companies they've backed. Read blog posts they've written, articles they've been quoted in, and their career history on sites like LinkedIn.

Pitching Isn't Free

Because investors see a lot of opportunities, they can look for familiar patterns across them. When you pitch a knowledgeable investor, if nothing else, you come away with some provocative questions and great insights. But you can also waste a lot of time pitching investors who aren't a good match for *your* business. Pitching isn't free: it costs you time. What's more, if you pitch too many investors, your deal becomes "shopped" and thus hard to sell.

I remember that when we were fundraising for our first company, we spent countless hours pitching venture investors. After a while, the questions the investors asked and the feedback we received were more or less the same. Although it was critical that we raise capital, we weren't spending that valuable time in the office working on the product or talking to customers.

All that pitching was exhausting! It reinforced for us the key challenges we faced and reminded us where we needed to focus. But it didn't provide insight into ways to build a great product, nor did it help solve any of the difficult questions we faced. Given our stage, the best source of capital for us was angel investors—investors who were betting primarily on us as a team that could figure out the business. And given our resources, the best use of our time was to pitch a few people and then get back to focusing on building the business and getting those tough questions answered.

I'll never forget the day we met with a potential partner in between a bunch of investor meetings. We started to give the product demo, and it didn't work. We'd been so busy meeting with investors that we had completely neglected the product. Had we not reset our priorities and gotten back to product focus, our time mismanagement could easily have caused our company to fail.

Investor Motivations: Greed and Fear

A huge part of pitching comes down to psychology and emotion. Investors are primarily motivated by two emotions: greed and fear. An investor who has access to invest in a hot company wants to buy as much of that company as possible. That investor is motivated by greed. Another classic example of the greedy investor is one who votes to turn down a big acquisition offer because the investor believes the company can be even more valuable. Of course, greed-based gambles sometimes pay off.

Investors operating out of fear worry they're going to lose a great deal or that a company they've already invested in will go out of business.

When you're pitching investors, it's easy to fall into the trap of *selling*. You're selling your company, your vision, and the opportunity to invest. The investor decides when and where to meet and may seem unmotivated by time. Meanwhile, you're trying to pay the bills, hire people, and generate revenue.

In fact, you want to be *buying*. Viewed through an extreme lens, you have a highly differentiated product—your company. All the investor has to offer is capital. If you've ever compared two $20 bills side by side, you can see how undifferentiated that capital is. Other than a difference in dates and serial numbers, those bills are just about the same!

Of course, investors are very different. They can offer access to a network of future capital, employees, and potentially better liquidity options down the line. But when pitching, it's easy to fall into the trap of only selling. Make sure you're buying good investors as well.

What does it mean to be buying? It means qualifying your investors. Investors are in the habit of asking lots of questions. You should ask qualification questions to get your investors to pitch you.

You must do this for several reasons:

- *The answers are important*: Without asking questions, it's hard to disqualify investors as potentially wrong for your startup.

- *It frames the discussion*: It puts you on equal footing with your investors; instead of one-way communication with you pitching and answering questions, you have a conversation, a dialog in which both parties are deciding whether to work with each other.

- *It plays to the emotional and psychological needs of your investors, not just the logical ones*: You want to motivate your investors through emotion. Greed drives up the price of your deal. Fear of losing the opportunity to invest incents investors to move quickly.

If these tactics seem artificial, they're not. They're a very real part of raising money for your company. They're the same tactics other successful entrepreneurs use to raise money. They're the tactics existing investors use to get future investors to invest. Without them, you won't be able to fund your company, and your company will fail. They're not just tactics—they're a key part of the strategy for making your company a success.

Process Matters

When it comes to pitching, it's important to manage the process, not just the product. If you line up one investor meeting for the beginning of April and another one for the beginning of May, you're not optimizing your investment process. Due to the amount of time between the meetings, you can't create a competitive situation between the investors. Nor can you easily pull them together if you want them both to invest. And it's difficult to compare them—you'll be well down the path or finished with one before you meet with the other. Line up investor meetings as close together as possible.

Entrepreneur X managed the investment process well. He had previously raised a small amount of money from some investors who backed him before. Having made some progress in the business, he went out for a full venture round, raising $10 million. Most considered the price guidance the entrepreneur was giving for the deal—a pre-money[1] valuation of $50 million—to be extremely high.

Yet Entrepreneur X ran a great process. He lined up nearly all of his investor meetings during a two-week period. For those who came later, he specifically went out of his way to tell them that they were running behind—feeding their fear that they might lose the deal before they had even figured out whether they wanted to invest.

His approach injected a lot of emotion into the process. Investor conversations around the merits and drawbacks of the deal took a back seat to discussions of how to win the deal. Entrepreneur X also masterfully started and finished every discussion with a potential investor with a statement about what he was looking for in an investor. He framed every conversation so that he was buying—not selling. Not only did Entrepreneur X get his deal done, and done quickly, but he got an even higher price than he wanted: a $58M pre-money valuation, raising $12M from investors.

Another reason to make your pitch process short and sweet is to prevent a *shopped* deal. Even though you may not have pitched a particular investor before, if you've pitched a lot of people, the investor has likely heard about your opportunity through a colleague or friend. That investor is already biased by whatever their colleague told them, even if they try not to be.

What's more, deals that have been around a long time feel tired. They get the taint of not being able to raise money, a taint that is very, very hard to remove. Because venture investors invest primarily in hope, not value, if a deal is *shopped*, it loses that shiny gleam of hope. Having an old and tired deal is a surefire recipe for pitching failure.

Vision First, Execution Second

Some early-stage investors look for vision. When they hear your pitch, they think even bigger, imagining what your company could become or how it could transform an industry. They immediately begin generating new ideas and talking about how big your opportunity could be.

---

[1] The pre-money valuation refers to the value of the company prior to the money (the investors' capital) being invested.

Other investors focus on operational excellence. They're all about the numbers. They want market data, acquisition metrics, and conversion rates.

Some of this is a factor of the stage of your business; the more revenue you have, the more likely it is that investors will focus on operational metrics over vision. But much of it depends on the personality of the investor.

Investors come with biases. All too frequently, experienced investors have been burned on an investment that appears similar to yours, which colors their view of your company. Alternatively, they may have missed an investment and spent years beating themselves up about it; when you arrive, they see not just your company, but a chance to redeem themselves for the investment they missed all those moons ago.

In the same week, I have pitched investors who were all about vision and others who were all about operational metrics. It's not that the operational investors didn't care about our vision—they did, at least to some extent. They simply were far more practical and, by their own admission, lacked the imagination of the vision-oriented investors. They had a much harder time envisioning a world-changing play and tended to make investments based on metrics.

Conversely, it's not that the vision-oriented investors didn't care about our operating metrics. They did. In fact, at least one of them was a previous serial entrepreneur and proven operating executive. But the vision investors cared a whole lot more about the market opportunity and were betting on us as a team to "figure it out."

Their biggest questions were around whether we had inherent biases that would prevent us from trying out diverse experiments on the path to scaling user and customer acquisition. In other words, were we willing to try many different approaches aggressively, some of them radical, until we figured out the ones that worked?

Of course, all vision with no metrics means you're building a house of cards. All metrics with no vision, and you may build a good business, but you won't get paid well for building it.

Investors want you to paint a picture of how you'll scale efficiently—that is, acquire and delight lots of users or customers. Or they want to know that you're already scaling, and that the invested capital will help you grow faster.

They need to convince themselves that you can, at some time in the future, extract more value from your users or customers than it costs you to acquire them. Note that I say "at some time in the future." Early-stage investors recognize that it may take a long time and a lot of capital before you reach profitability—in fact, they may no longer be investors in the company by the time that happens. But they need to be able to convince themselves (and others) that there is a path to get there.

Spell It Out

Many pitches fail because they leave big chunks of the pitch as an exercise for the reader. Don't expect your investors to reach the same conclusions you would based on your data, analysis, or a product demo. Instead, draw the conclusions for them.

If you tell potential investors your market is really big but you don't tell them how you'll reach that market, they may come away believing your market is really big. But they're left wondering how you'll reach it efficiently.

Addressing key issues like this not only requires that you think about them, which is a good thing, but also demonstrates that you have done so. Investors tend to assume the best about opportunity and the worst about risk.

Show them a big market opportunity, and they will think even bigger. Fail to show them how you'll reach that market, and they will assume the worst—that the market is unreachable or that you have no idea how to reach it.

You Are the Product

When you're pitching to customers, your product is a piece of software or hardware, a service, or a web site. When you're pitching investors, *you* are the product. And just as you need to find product-market fit for the software, hardware, or service you're building, you also need to find product-market fit when *you* are the product.

It may seem obvious, but a pitch isn't just about the content. You're evaluating your potential investors based on the questions they ask, the knowledge they demonstrate about your space and approach, and their networks. Meanwhile, your investors are evaluating the entire product that is you: the market opportunity, your strategy for capturing that opportunity, and you and your team.

Many entrepreneurs fail at pitching because they make incredibly basic mistakes. They don't demonstrate knowledge of what they're doing and confidence when pitching. As Admiral Greer told Jack Ryan in *The Hunt for Red October*, "No one understands this material better than you do."

When investors evaluate you, they're evaluating whether you

- Present effectively

- Can recruit, sell, and communicate a big vision

- Know more about your domain than anyone else

- Think strategically

- Have ambition (are you building something big or small?)

- Are a great fundraiser

That last bullet may seem a little bit of a chicken-and-egg problem. But part of what investors are evaluating is whether they think other investors will want to give you more money in the future.

Investors know that most businesses ultimately require more capital. They don't want to be in it alone and are already thinking about how the market will view you the next time you go out to raise money.

Saying things like "this is the last money we'll ever need," when you're not doing tens or hundreds of millions in revenue demonstrates ignorance.

Perfect Your Pitch

Not only are you a product, your pitch is a product too. Although every pitch is different, there are five key elements to focus on when you pitch:

1. Framing and personal status

2. Your vision

3. That your category will be big, and the time is now

4. How you'll reach the market, scale, and become the leader

5. Why what you're doing is valuable and strategic

Framing Sets the Context

Tons of pitches fail every day due to bad framing. Fundraiser and author of *Pitch Anything*, Oren Klaff, writes that "framing" is one of the most important activities that separates good pitches from bad ones. With good framing, you set the right context for your interactions with potential investors and create equal status for your discussions.

You don't need to be arrogant about your approach, but a little hotness goes a long way. Like it or not, raising money can be a bit of a high-school popularity contest, and status plays a big role. As one investor friend of mine is fond of saying about pitching, it often comes down to, "I'm hot, you're hot, let's be hot together."

Cliché as it may sound, pitching is a lot like dating. One amazing fundraiser once said (he was European), "We will romance them." And it was true. He did romance investors, and they fell in love with his vision and dream.

Framing starts long before your meeting. It starts with how you handle your availability and communication with potential investors. You cannot—you must not—be needy. If you're sitting in a meeting room and your investors are running late, giving them a few minutes is no big deal. But don't sit around waiting for more than 15 minutes.

Be polite about it, but reschedule. Ask yourself if you really want to be in business with someone who starts off treating you with that kind of lack of respect. I know the feeling—it was incredibly hard to secure that meeting, and it's been rescheduled. But you must drive respect. People are on time for things that are important to them.

Similarly, don't overstay your welcome. Set the expectation at the beginning of the meeting that you need to leave a few minutes early for another important meeting. Of course, you would be happy to schedule more time if that makes sense after the initial meeting.

This does two things. First, it sets the right tone for the meeting—your time is important, and you're in demand. Second, it lets the investor respond with their availability as well; perhaps their schedule has changed.

As the old saying goes, don't sell past the close. You have a lot of work to do—recruiting, building great product, acquiring users or customers, marketing, and so on. Your time is critically valuable.

If you have an hour scheduled for your meeting with an investor, prepare to leave ten minutes before that hour is up. If you want to spend more time and they want to spend more time, don't worry—there will be plenty more meetings to come.

Avoid that all-too-frequent awkward moment when the investor's assistant walks in and tells the investor, "Joe is on the line," or "Your next meeting is here." Be the first to stand up and make ready to leave. And then do just that—leave! Again, there will be more meetings if you intend to do business together.

I have had entrepreneurs ask me, "So, what are the next steps?" and, "Tell me, honestly, what do you think?" In many business meetings, the goal is to get to action items so the meeting will have been productive. That is *not* the goal of a pitch meeting. It isn't a mystery what the action items and next steps are from a pitch meeting: more meetings, then a term sheet that spells out the terms of the deal, and then a wire transfer to your bank account.

Moreover, it may be OK to ask for direct feedback one to one. But if you're in a group setting, where you're pitching multiple people in the room, you introduce an unnecessary risk of failure when you ask for immediate feedback. Not only do you appear needy, but you also throw yourself into the deep end of a pool of group dynamics with which you're completely unfamiliar.

You have very little idea what the relationships are among the people on the other side of the table and what the dynamics of the investment firm are. Who carries weight on investment decisions? How does the group handle disagreements about deals and associated feedback? Are there portfolio management issues that could impact investing in your deal?

Are the people on the other side of the table comfortable giving candid feedback in a group setting? Or would your contact prefer to talk with you one to one? The level of variability is incredibly high and something you have little visibility into and control over.

I have sat through pitch meetings where entrepreneurs mismanaged their time. They spent too much time on things that weren't relevant to a decision about whether to have a second meeting, such as minute details of a product or financial plan. They simply ran out of time.

In cases where I or other investors tried to alert entrepreneurs that they were running out of time, many have tried to go faster but kept the same level of detail. This is a sure-fire recipe for failure. Instead, bump up a level and cover the important points. Save the rest for a second meeting.

Investors who are interested follow up. They make introductions, connect you with people, and generally try to act helpful. An investor who is really interested tries to suck up all your available time. That way, no other investors can spend time with you until the investor decides whether to do the deal. And if your deal is really hot, you may even experience that rare phenomenon, "Don't let that guy leave the building."

The negotiation for your deal starts long before you talk terms. How you frame from the very beginning impacts the tenor of your negotiation. Act needy and reschedule your life around potential investors, and you indicate low status in the relationship. In the remote chance that they still want to do your deal, they know they can not only beat you up on price; they can control your company as well.

Presentation Failure

Whether or not the oft-quoted statistic that 93% of communication is nonverbal is accurate, how you communicate during a pitch, both verbally and nonverbally, matters a lot.

Just the other day, a few entrepreneurs were running through their presentation with me. They had a great pitch, a great team, and a big market. The only problem was, they didn't look at me while they talked. I remember another pitch where an executive spent the entire presentation looking down at the conference table. It was very awkward.

If you pitch poorly, potential investors ask themselves: if you can't communicate your vision clearly to me (the investor), why would I think you'll be able to communicate it to your own team? And if you can't communicate with your own employees to set direction, how will you get anything done? The answer is—you won't.

Many entrepreneurs face two key challenges when presenting. First, they have trouble making and holding eye contact. Second, they have trouble being succinct.

Connect With Your Audience

Having trouble connecting with your audience is understandable. Many product people spend a lot of time in front of their computers. Computers don't stare back, move around, grimace, smile, go in and out of the room, check their mobile devices, or get distracted. In fact, they don't respond much at all (except occasionally to let you know they've crashed and need to restart). It's for this very reason that, consciously or subconsciously, many entrepreneurs with engineering and product backgrounds have chosen to work with computers.

As a result, communicating a vision in person, one to one or in a group, may not be second nature. Some entrepreneurs fail to make eye contact with their audience while pitching. They look down, they look away, they do just about anything but communicate with their audience.

Others suffer from what I call the "warm coffee comfort" problem. It's one thing to take a sip of water so your throat doesn't dry out. It's another to coddle a warm cup of coffee or tea, in what is clearly a comfort mechanism. You'd be surprised how many people do this—it's both distracting and confidence reducing.

Instead of looking at their audience, some people look at their slides, projected or displayed on a screen behind them, while they present. They talk to the screen instead of to the people in the room. Some go so far as to turn their back on their audience, and a few stand with the projector light beaming directly into their eyes.

People who are great at presenting become that way by practicing. But in the absence of having years to practice, following a few simple presentation rules can go a long way. These are rules you can easily see in action in YouTube videos on presenting:

- *Make eye contact:* Not short and sudden, but steady. Don't jump around the room. Some people find making eye contact uncomfortable. It makes them feel awkward, or they worry about coming across as intimidating or staring. Whatever the reason, if you find making eye contact uncomfortable, use the old trick of looking at people's eyebrows or just above their nose. It's not perfect, but it's a very functional quick fix.

- *Keep your eyes in the horizontal plane:* Look around, not down.

- *Face the person you're addressing with your body:* Talking to someone isn't just about making eye contact—it's about facing them with your body.

- *Stand up:* It's hard to pitch seated. It contracts your lung capacity and makes it more challenging to be expressive.

- *Don't pace, and don't lean on chairs:* It's distracting.

- *Use humor:* You don't need to be a comedian, but if people laugh because you've said something funny, enjoy the moment. A little humor builds a lot of rapport.

- *Breathe:* Take a breath. Many entrepreneurs rush through their pitches, and when they run short on time, they talk even faster. Breathe more, say less.

- *Know your material and the messages you want to leave people with:* You don't need to read your slides if you know what's on them.

- *Acknowledge your co-founder or other executives, and hand off to them:* It's often hard for people to introduce themselves in a big room. Instead, demonstrate you're a team with the simple words, "And now I'd like to hand things off to my co-founder…" or words to that effect. If it helps, visualize the hand-off as passing the football—you've made the pass, your partner has received it, and now you can continue to move the ball down the field.

Employing a speaker coach can help a lot. However, coaches often focus on details. Don't try to change who you are. Instead, practice facing people, looking at them, breathing, handing off to your colleagues, and coming back to your concise, key messages. Minimize distractions. Do that, and you'll be 90% of the way there.

Be Succinct

Now for the other 90%. Be succinct. When investors, potential board members, or people you're talking to ask you a question about your business, provide a crisp, direct answer.

Engineers, especially, have a tendency to go deeper and give more detail rather than bumping up a level and talking about the big picture. Quite often when investors ask questions they're not looking for long, drawn-out explanations. They're evaluating how you respond as much as the specific content of your answer. In a group of people, if you dive into a lengthy explanation of how your product works, for example, you may connect with one person, but you'll likely lose the interest of others.

Many presenters tend to provide a long explanation and then provide the answer. Just give the answer right away—you may as well, since you're going to give it anyway. Then explain. Spend time with the best executives and leaders and you'll notice they excel at "netting it out." They cut to the core of big issues. Do the same and you'll come out ahead.

Back to our entrepreneurs. While they started out seeming nervous and a bit disconnected, after working on connecting with their audience and being succinct they came across as a confident team. They aced their pitches. So will you.

Expect Due Diligence

Due diligence is the process during which investors dig into the details of your opportunity—the market, the competition, your metrics, and your team.

I remember one diligence call that was a reference on the founder of a company. The person I was calling was genuinely surprised to hear from me. Granted, I made the call the same day I got the reference list from the founder. But the founder had neglected to tell him that investors might be calling. That wasn't a reason not to do the deal, but it certainly felt odd.

Contrast that with the entrepreneur who had been well-coached. He offered to provide references, but only after I'd made some progress on other diligence aspects like market and competition. I took no offense at this. Rather, it demonstrated that he valued his references and didn't want to overuse them, and also that he was testing me to see how serious I was about investing.

There is a saying among investors that during diligence, a deal loses altitude, and the question is whether it will regain it. During diligence, investors come face to face with the incredible number of risks associated with a deal. They have to overcome those risks and potentially convince their partners, if they're part of a larger fund, that they and the company have an approach to mitigating those risks.

Support Your Sponsor

To get through due diligence, it pays to get on the same side as your sponsor. Your sponsor, at any investment shop bigger than one individual, is the champion who shepherds you through the firm and "owns" the deal. No matter how in-demand your deal is, you want to help that person execute an investment in your company. After all, you never know when you'll need a stalking horse.

That means helping your sponsor pull together the investment memo, slides, and diligence materials. It doesn't mean bending over backward or in any way compromising the mutual respect that goes into the best entrepreneur-investor partnerships.

The most effective way to do this is to sit down with your sponsor and have a candid discussion about how the process works at your sponsor's firm. This isn't a discussion of the details of your opportunity. Rather, it's a brief discussion about the investment process—on your side and theirs.

How are investment decisions made? What materials will the sponsor be pulling together? This brief process discussion is yet another opportunity for you to frame and reframe your relationship and the potential partnership you're entering into with the investor. In addition to asking questions, you should take the opportunity to talk about activities that need to take place and are taking place on your end.

One major item is to begin speaking with CEOs of the investor's portfolio companies to get a sense for how the firm interacts with its founders and CEOs. Among other things, you want to know how the firm deals with follow-on investments and handles companies that need more capital to reach their objectives. This is useful and valuable information.

You can also communicate—even if unasked—where you are in the process with other investors. Assuming that multiple investors are actively in diligence, you want to make sure those who are genuinely interested have time to do the work they need to do; but you also want to communicate that your deal is in demand.

By having these kinds of discussions, you continue to frame your relationship. Your message is that it's not just a question of whether the investor wants to invest in you. It's equally a question of whether you want to take that investor's money.

Understand Partner Meetings

If you're raising venture capital, at some point you'll come in contact with a Monday partner meeting. Partner meetings typically take place on Mondays at just about every venture-capital firm (although some firms are known for holding Sunday night partner meetings to preempt the competition when there is a hot deal to be won). A partner meeting is when all the partners at a firm get together to discuss firm business and ongoing financings, and hear the pitches of new companies as a group.

When a company comes in to present, the sponsor typically has already circulated a deal memo, a capital planning model (CPM), a copy of the presentation the entrepreneur will present, and relevant diligence notes and industry material. Depending on the stature of your sponsor, you can expect more or less process, preparation, and material.

The deal memo describes the opportunity, risks, team, and financing in detail. The CPM models capital needs of the company and expected return. The other information provides additional context. The sponsor may give a brief presentation or overview before the company presents.

A partner meeting isn't the time to get bogged down in gory details. It's an opportunity to paint your vision, get people excited, and demonstrate complete command of what you're doing, from market to execution. The most important thing you can do in a partner meeting is to be highly engaged. Give your pitch, and don't overstay. Demonstrate that yours is a deal people should be excited about. Show that although you're excited about the prospect of working with the firm in question, yours is a deal they need to win if they want to work with you.

A friend of the firm may sit in on your presentation and provide the partnership with a perspective on your deal and on your market. In most cases, you'll have met that person during diligence. Don't sweat it.

After you leave the room, your sponsor will talk about the opportunity, risks, risk mitigation, and financing. The partnership will discuss the opportunity.

Partnerships have different structures for deciding how deals get done. Some follow a sponsor/devil's advocate model, where one partner is the champion and another is the designated devil's advocate. Other partnerships require a sponsor and co-sponsor. Some require unanimity or the vote of at least one managing partner.

In some partnerships, it's a foregone conclusion that a deal coming into a Monday partner meeting will get done. Other partnerships may see two or three new deals on a Monday and choose to do only one—or none—of them. What's important is to be focused, engaged, in control of your material, and in demand. Remember, you're not just selling; you're buying.

A recipe for failure is to bring your whole team with you, mismanage your time, and demonstrate a lack of command of your material. You should bring at the very most three people, in the case of a multifounder company.

Think big. Be succinct. Get to the point when answering questions. And, because you've managed the investment process to perfection—get on over to your next Monday meeting!

Summary

Pitching investors takes a lot of time and energy. To succeed at pitching you need to:

- Pitch investors that are appropriate for your business.

- Get investors excited about what you're doing and your ability to transform, recruit, and raise capital.

- Be in command of your material.

- Not *need* the money, or at least credibly give the impression that you don't need the money.

Buy, don't just sell. The right entrepreneur-investor combination can truly be a partnership. You'll be in business with your investors for a long time. Find the partnership that's right for you.

CHAPTER 11

Managing Liquidity

Get Paid for Your Work

Inexperienced sellers leave money on the table all the time. One investor I know once told me, "We're going to get the vacuum cleaner out and suck all the money off the table. Then, we're going to stick that vacuum into their pockets and make sure we've got every last cent." Needless to say, his words left a lasting impression. Although you may not come from the Vacuum Cleaner Investor school of deals, there's no reason not to get paid for your work.

Liquidity Events

When I was first starting out, I met a very successful entrepreneur who told me, "I never met an acquisition offer I didn't like." I thought this guy was nuts. What was the point of starting a company if we were just going to be bought? We were going public, and that was the end of that. Of course, it was late 2000, and the public markets had all but completely dried up.

The reality is, 90% of liquidity events are acquisitions, not IPOs. For a tech company to go public, the IPO window has to be open, institutional buyers—known as the *buy side*—have to be interested, and the company must meet key metrics, such as specific revenue levels and sustained growth rates. The management team has to be able to credibly sell the story. And the company must have avoided being acquired along the way. After all, many of the same characteristics that make a company attractive to the public markets also make it attractive to other, larger companies. Those companies often seek to augment organic growth with growth via acquisitions.

You put all the hard work into your startup well before a liquidity event takes place. But how you manage the liquidity process can have a dramatic effect on how others value all that hard work. Just as with private fundraising, the environment surrounding the liquidity event can have a significant impact on your company's valuation as well.

Big companies are experts at buying smaller companies. That doesn't mean they're always (or even often) wise at choosing those acquisitions or good at integrating them once acquired.

But it does mean they've been through the process hundreds, if not thousands, of times. Some acquisitions are tiny—say, a small group of engineers bought for their team and technology. Others are huge mergers of near-equals. Big companies have in-house legal teams, in addition to outside counsel; corporate development departments responsible for deal execution; and, typically, a business owner who drives the desire for an acquisition to occur.

The art of the deal is to know when to say "no" and when to say "yes." Sell too easily or to the wrong buyer, and the value of years of hard work can evaporate in an instant. But the first question you should ask yourself is: do you want to be bought?

Don't assume that your potential acquirers know your company—especially if your company is smaller. The delicate art of getting bought is that you're not for sale. But you do need to be visible—highly visible. You need to be on the radar of potential acquirers. That means being visible in the press and at conferences, spreading the word about your company through your network, and personally getting to know people at those companies that might acquire you.

One entrepreneur I know took a strategic investment from a much larger company. Although it prevented him from running out of money and gave him a partner to work with, other potential acquirers viewed the startup as already spoken for. That is, by investing a relatively small (for them) amount of money in the startup, the big company effectively owned the startup without having to buy it outright.

The entrepreneur and his team kept having to deliver on the demands of their strategic partner to such an extent that they didn't have the bandwidth to serve the rest of the market.

The entrepreneur considered breaking the contract with the larger company multiple times, but the startup had become so dependent on the larger company that changing course was impractical. One of the startup's competitors eventually acquired it, providing little return.

Another entrepreneur took a much different approach. He started with a business partnership with a potential acquirer that involved marketing their products together. It took a lot of effort on the startup's part to make the relationship productive—the bigger company had lots of other partners.

Ironically, the first partnership led to partnerships with other large companies in the industry, one of which eventually bought the startup. By managing and finessing these business relationships, the entrepreneur was able to capitalize on them from a marketing perspective without becoming encumbered by them.

Why Acquisitions Fail to Go Through

There are a number of reasons acquisitions fail to go through, many of which can be avoided with proper planning. Becoming visible, building relationships, and engaging with multiple potential acquirers are all activities that take time and preparation.

Selling, Not Buying

As with many of the other business transactions discussed earlier in the book, the best deals are those in which you're buying, not selling. That means the best acquisitions occur when someone wants to buy you when you aren't actively selling.

But often, companies that are short on capital are trying to sell. Investors, management, or both may be tired. Many deals fail to go through because the CEOs are trying too hard to sell the deal. They may end up with a sale, but it's frequently for a low-ball price that could have been avoided.

Not Being on the Radar

One CEO had the networking skills of a hermit. A talented inside guy, well-liked and respected by his team, he didn't excel at networking. As a result, his company didn't get the call when larger companies pursued acquisitions in his space. His potential deals failed because they never got started.

The reality is that he didn't want to sell. Although his company was growing very slowly and not becoming more valuable, he enjoyed the relatively comfortable position the company was in and his role as CEO. He had previously been a senior executive at a large, public tech company and wasn't eager to take on a similar role.

Lack of Relationship

Not dissimilar from this was another CEO who, although a great product guy, was so disinterested that he failed to connect with the teams at potential acquirers. He entered into multiple potential acquisition discussions, but was outmaneuvered twice by other CEOs who had better relationships.

There is no substitute for having a longstanding business relationship with someone, but relationships are built over time. You may have worked with someone in a previous job or gone to school together, or you may be neighbors. The relationship-lacking CEO placed very low value on relationships and as a result failed to get engagement with potential acquirers, even though some of them were genuinely interested in buying his company.

Acquirer Strategic Shift

One CEO's deal was put on hold when the Senior VP sponsor at the company that was going to acquire him changed roles. In a cliché blame game, investors argued that the CEO should have had his finger on the pulse of the acquirer so he wasn't blindsided by the change.

Although they're often slow to move, large companies change strategies and reprioritize frequently. They defund projects and reorganize departments and divisions. Sometimes sponsors are blindsided by CEO or board-level directives, other executives, or market changes. Other times, they either don't have their ducks in a row or don't command sufficient influence to get a deal done.

That said, it pays to get to know all the potential players at an acquirer, not just your direct sponsor. Other groups or executives may feel threatened by the prospect of their company acquiring yours, or they may suffer from NIH—not invented here syndrome—in which they believe they can do whatever you're doing better by building it internally. Ultimately, however, it's your responsibility to know as much as possible about what's going on with your sponsor, other players, and your potential acquirers.

Expectation Mismatch

The CEO of Company X repeatedly turned down offers because management and investor expectations about price and deal terms didn't match those of potential acquirers. The CEO of the company was operationally excellent but didn't paint a strategic vision that an acquiring team could buy into to justify his and his investors' lofty valuation expectations. As a result, the company was valued purely on a multiple of its revenue rather than viewed as a critical, must-have, strategic acquisition.

In particular, the CEO of Company X failed to help each potential acquirer understand why his company was a possible cornerstone of an existing strategic initiative the larger company had underway—one of the best ways to get a higher-value outcome. The CEO failed to frame discussions properly from the beginning because he focused purely on the numbers rather than on the strategic needs of potential acquirers.

As much as executives feel pressure to beat the numbers, many feel just as much pressure to "be someone." CEOs of companies, large and small, want to be successful and want to be known for that success. It's not only about money. It's also about power and ego. No CEO wants to go down in history as an unstrategic, failed leader. Most want to be recognized not only for having driven growth but also for having been great leaders. Not only did the CEO of Company X fail to invest in the strategic vision of his potential acquirers—he also failed to understand how he could help his sponsors and their CEOs be stars.

In contrast, the CEO of Company Y, with just a few million in revenue, was able to sell his company for hundreds of millions of dollars. Both companies were in spaces where larger companies were incredibly acquisitive, but the more-strategic CEO went to great pains to understand the strategies and initiatives of his potential acquirers. When he met with executives at a potential acquirer, he didn't only talk operations—he talked about the acquirer's key strategic needs. What's more, acting as a peer, but without being arrogant, he had candid conversations with senior executives about their challenges in the organization. He knew so much about his potential acquirers' businesses and about the executives themselves that they asked him for his input on their plans. When one of the companies decided it needed to make an acquisition, he was the first person they called.

Lack of a Competitive Bidding Situation

This is by far the most painful cause of deal failure and nearly ensures you won't get an optimal price. It also makes it regrettably easy to become emotionally attached to a particular acquirer. If things are going well and a company is in high demand, getting into a competitive bidding situation is easy.

The challenge, of course, is getting a competitive bidding situation going when a company is running short on cash and needs money quickly. Big companies are always sniffing around for technologies and teams they can acquire on the cheap. If they sense tired capital or tired management, they'll toss in a lowball offer on the off chance it will be accepted.

Tired investors and management, operating in fear mode, are eerily susceptible to low-ball offers. If you have investors, the dance is an especially delicate one. Some investors may be willing to chip in more capital to help buy you time until you get a deal done. Others may have already written off your company. Find out where they are early in the process so you're not surprised.

Lack of Chemistry

The CEO of Company Y had a personality issue. Although multiple larger companies wanted to buy his company for hundreds of millions of dollars, his personality got in the way of the deals getting done. Some people called him antagonistic; others described him as always having to be the smartest guy in the room. He never failed to show up the employees and executives of potential acquirers. Although acquiring his business made sense from a business perspective, acquirers decided they couldn't work with the CEO. Failing to swallow his pride personally cost him tens of millions of dollars. After three such failed acquisition discussions, his investors brought in a new CEO.

Hiring Employees Instead

This is an age-old tactic of ruthless acquirers: rather than buy the company, hire some of the key employees. More than one CEO has been known to say, "These guys would never do that," only later to come to a board meeting saying, "Those bastards! They're trying to hire my best people!" If you're entering into serious discussions, it isn't unusual to specify a no-hire provision in your memorandum of understanding (MOU) with the potential acquirer.

Granted, the provision may not be enforceable, and it's not likely you'll spend the time or money to take serious legal action. However, it allows you to have the discussion and set the expectation up front that you won't tolerate bad behavior. It also gives you strong moral high ground to fall back on, should your acquirer try to hire any of your employees while you're engaged in discussions or shortly thereafter.

Due-Diligence Issues

Some acquisition discussions fall apart during diligence. In exchange for capital very early on, the founder of Company Z entered into a license agreement with another company that gave that company the right to use Company Z's technology in a different market segment. As it was structured, the business partner had rights to all future versions of Company Z's technology. Although Company Z was almost acquired, the deal failed because more than one potential acquirer didn't want to take on the obligation of having to provide updates to the business partner.

Over the next year, the founder of Company Z restructured the contractual relationship with his business partner. He convinced the partner that encumbered by the unlimited license agreement, Company Z might not be able to sustain its business, and so it was in the business partner's best interests to restructure the relationship. That, combined with some financial incentives the founder put in place to compensate the business partner in the event Company Z was acquired, enabled Company Z to restructure the contract. Free and clear to operate, the founder of Company Z decided not to sell. Instead, he raised an additional $14 million in venture capital to scale the business.

Getting the Deal Done

Anyone who has been through an acquisition (or acquisition discussions) has been faced with more than a few roomfuls of the acquirer's people—sometimes a roomful of executives, other times a roomful of engineers, finance, or legal people—or a mix of all of the above.

Many acquirers try to extract as much information as possible from you and your team during acquisition discussions. Some are on fishing expeditions, trying to pick your brain to inform their strategy. Others know they want to make an acquisition in a particular space but don't know which company or companies they want to buy. Although you'll ultimately end up disclosing a lot of information if things get serious, it's critical to have checkpoints at every step of the way.

As with investment discussions, framing is crucial in acquisition discussions. Don't just ask how things are looking on the acquirer's end—if you do, you'll be selling, not buying. Instead, let them know how things are looking on your end and that you have some concerns—now you're buying, and getting the acquirer selling you on why they're the right buyer for your company.

Although it can feel flattering to have a big company approach you and to be in meetings with employees of that company, there is no need to divulge too much detail before both sides are ready to engage in serious discussions.

Understand the players, what their goals are, and what your goals are, for every meeting and every communiqué. Think of every interaction as both content (what are you learning, and what are they learning?) and signaling (what messages are they sending you, and what messages are you sending them?). Silence, of course, can be a very powerful message. You can also leverage your board, as in, "Joe, our board won't budge on that issue." However you pursue a deal, figure out what you care about. Don't be deceived by the offer of a big title, flattery, or wining and dining.

Understand who the key decision-makers are, and get to know all of them. Get clarity on the acquisition process. Whether that turns out to be the actual process or not, it gives you something you can hold the acquirer to when discussions speed up, slow down, or stall.

Failing to Get Paid

Given the right situation, *everything* about a liquidity event is negotiable. When it comes to an acquisition, the purchase price itself, the deal terms, your earn-out, your compensation (and termination) package, and benefits at the new company are all up for discussion. You can even carve out technology or intellectual property that may not be relevant to the acquirer so you can do something else with it in the future. On the other hand, getting too fancy can kill a deal.

Earn-outs are compensation that management and employees receive separate from the purchase itself. They're frequently based on hitting specific *future* revenue or profitability targets. They can also be very deceiving. More than one management team has taken what seemed like a huge earn-out, only to find out later that they and their acquirer had different understandings of how the earn-out would be calculated.

Take, for example, an earn-out based on hitting certain revenue targets. The first question to consider is how those revenue targets were set. In all likelihood, the acquirer asked you for three- or five-year financial projections. The minute you handed those over, you were setting—perhaps unknowingly—a critical component of your earn-out.

The second question is how much control you'll have over hitting your revenue goals, after the acquisition takes place. Your product might depend on direct sales. Suppose that all post-acquisition sales must be made by the acquirer's existing sales force. That sales force must be educated about your product, learn how to sell it, and be incented to sell it—assuming they're equipped to sell it at all.

Profit-based earn-out goals are even more challenging. Until you spend significant time with a company's CFO, you don't know for sure how expenses are allocated across the organization. You may also find that the cost of salaries and benefits the acquirer pays are significantly higher than what you were paying as a startup—thereby driving up all the costs that go into your profitability metrics.

Although you may be on the same page as your acquirer during the deal process, things can change quickly post acquisition. Prior to being at a company, you have relatively limited visibility into what the company is really like, no matter how much time you spend with executives and employees there. What's more, big companies go through reorganizations and restructurings all the time. The business owner who did your deal may switch roles or go work somewhere else. The CFO who talked you through the numbers may be fired. The CEO who told you everything you wanted to hear while the deal was getting done may be a completely different person to work for.

Many seemingly successful acquisitions have turned into financial failures for entrepreneurs after the deals were consummated. The best way to avoid that kind of failure is by working out the specifics, in detail, before your deal closes.

Secondary Markets and Interim Liquidity

Liquidity can and does occur before a company goes public or is acquired by another company. Sometimes, some portion of newly invested capital goes out the door. It's not used to fund the capital needs of the company but rather to provide liquidity for existing investors, founders, and employees. This kind of *founder liquidity* often occurs as part of a larger financing, but it can happen separately.

Proponents of founder liquidity argue that it helps entrepreneurs continue to take extreme risk because they have a nest egg. Opponents argue that it makes entrepreneurs less hungry and reduces alignment with investors. Invested capital should be used to fund the growth of the business, not line pockets. Regardless, this kind of liquidity occurs in some deals because the deals are so hot that founders can make participation in the financing contingent on them taking out some cash—in some cases, very significant amounts.

Secondary transactions have existed for years, but they have gained significant visibility recently due to the emergence of secondary marketplaces like SecondMarket and SharesPost. In these cases, the marketplace acts as an intermediary, lining up buyers and sellers. However, unlike public-market stocks, such transactions are only available to accredited investors (that is, investors who meet certain income or net worth requirements) or institutional funds. Although the number of transactions has grown, they occur in a relatively small universe of companies, typically those that are very well-known, such as Facebook.

People often ask why existing investors (also known as *insiders*) sell a portion of their ownership if they're still bullish on a company. A lot of it comes down to portfolio and fund management. By getting some early liquidity, an investor can reduce risk—although the upside is somewhat reduced, taking a small amount off the table mitigates the downside.

In addition to reducing risk, general partners in venture-capital funds derive some big benefits from small amounts of early liquidity. Whether they can *recycle* (that is, reinvest the capital) depends on the stage of the fund. But the bigger benefit is that they can return capital to their limited partners—those investors who invest in venture-capital funds. They can raise more money based on having already returned money, as in the old saying, "Success begets success." And, they can take some gains off the table.

IPOs

I won't spend a lot of time on initial public offerings (IPOs). If you're considering an IPO, you're surrounded by advisors, board members, bankers, and others who can help manage the process and coach you through it.

The CEOs I know who have gone from being private to public company CEOs consistently complain about one thing: the focus on short-term results. They may have new ideas or want to make major strategic changes, but the pressure to hit the number every quarter makes making big changes challenging.

Some of them, of course, use this as an excuse for not being able to hit the numbers they promised. But many are frustrated—not only do they have to contend with a large organization that has evolved over time, but they also must deal with public-market individual and institutional investors. Although it may sometimes not seem that way, private companies and their management teams have a lot more flexibility.

When Your Company Is the Product

Ultimately, great liquidity events are built on product-market fit. By this I don't mean building a technology product that users want to use or customers want to buy, although that, of course, is critical. I mean your company *is* the product, and the market consists of potential acquirers and the public markets.

A great liquidity event occurs when the product you're marketing—your company, with its vision, team, products, customers, revenue, growth trajectory, and other assets—matches the needs of a buyer who wants the product that is your company.

Summary

To achieve a great outcome:

- Plan your way to liquidity.
- Be bought, not sold.
- Get paid for your work.

From Failure, Success

Mistakes: The Stepping Stones to Startup Victory

Entrepreneurs start companies for many reasons. They can't or don't want to work for someone else. They enjoy the rush of knowing there's no one to point the finger at but themselves. They crave the attention. They want to be rich. Or they want to change the world. This chapter presents some key considerations to think about along the way and inform your decision whether to hold or sell. But ultimately, your personal aspirations determine what you should do. It's one thing to read about how to turn failure into success and another to experience it first-hand.

Many Motivations Fuel Entrepreneurship

The sacrifices involved in doing a startup are significant—long hours, high rates of failure, uncertainty about the future, and an extreme emotional roller-coaster ride. But the rewards are also significant and not just financial. There are lots of reasons to start a company.

You have a personal need you want to solve. You see a gap in the market. You want to have an impact. You like building products. You thrive on the dopamine rush when a user or customer tells you about a great experience with your product—and you know you personally made it happen.

You want to understand all aspects of business, from product to user acquisition to finance. You want to build your own team. You want more control over your future. You want to see your name on an IPO prospectus.

You want to be rich. You want to be famous. You can't get a job. You don't want to work for someone else. You want to get revenge on a previous company or boss. You hate big-company politics. You find making decisions and feeling their immediate impact rewarding. You thrive on challenges. You idolize Steve Jobs, Marc Benioff, Bill Gates, and Mark Zuckerberg, to name just a few. You've always been an entrepreneur and know no other path.

By building a consumer product, you can solve a problem you face and address a personal need—a need you may find that millions of other people have as well. If you build a business product, you can solve key customer problems, and you have the opportunity to transform and disrupt huge industries.

It's incredibly rewarding to build and sell something of value. When I was in middle school, I developed shareware programs. These were software programs that were free to use but required a nominal registration fee to get rid of annoying "Please register" reminder messages. I'll never forget the day I received my first check in the mail for $10.

On a Wednesday evening, after school, my Dad said, "There's an envelope here for you." He did his best to hide his concern. I opened the envelope.

"It's a check! A check for $10!" I exclaimed.

"For what?" His concern had shifted to surprise.

"For this software program I wrote!"

Someone—a person I had never met—considered the software program I built useful and sent me money for it. I was beyond elated. The checks started rolling in, first one a week, then two. I deposited them at the bank into my passbook savings account. This was a little book the size of a passport where the bank recorded every transaction—on paper!

One day, a few months later, I recall going to the bank with lots of checks in a manila envelope. I walked right up to the teller and emptied the checks onto the counter, dozens of them for $10 and $12—I had started raising prices when I realized I had a good thing going. The teller explained to me that my savings account had a limit on the number of transactions I could make per month. She sent me over to one of the bank managers (it was a small branch), who looked at me with a bemused smile.

"How can I help you, young man?"

"I want to deposit these checks." I once again emptied out the checks, this time onto the mahogany desk between me and the manager.

"Where did you get these?"

"From the people who sent them to me," I replied, rather taken aback. It seemed obvious to me.

"And what are they for?"

"For these software programs I wrote," I responded, motioning with my hands to indicate the (invisible) software programs. I got a highly skeptical look in reply. The manager stared at me as if trying to see the software programs.

Mysterious as the invisible software was, the manager wasn't about to break one of the cardinal rules of banking. If a customer has money to deposit, take it!

"Well, son, if you have checks to deposit, we need to get you set up with a checking account." And the rest, as they say, is history.

I had made money before, for shoveling snow and doing yard work. But I had never been paid repeatedly without having to do more work and with almost no physical goods or labor involved. Only years later would I come to appreciate how that translated into high margins, which translated into building a valuable business.

The Myth of Working for Yourself

I'll never forget the time one of my employees told me about his wife and his mortgage. He was a risk-taker, willing to work at a startup for below-market pay for the chance to do something big and game-changing. He put in 14-, 16-, and 18-hour days at work. But he was depending on us—the founders—to make the right decisions, both strategically and tactically, to build our little company into something big.

Until that point, I had seen startups as a romantic undertaking where we worked for ourselves. At that moment I realized we didn't work for ourselves at all. In fact, the bigger our company got, the less we worked for ourselves and the more we worked for other people.

We got to set our own direction, decide what to build and who to build it for, and operate out of self-motivation. People are fond of saying that entrepreneurs start companies so they can work for themselves. The reality is that as entrepreneurs, we don't truly work for ourselves. We work for our users and customers, our employees, and our investors.

Many entrepreneurs become disillusioned about their companies when they realize that not only don't they work for themselves, but they actually have many bosses.

Entrepreneur Y built a web site over a weekend. In a matter of months, he had hundreds of thousands of users. Many of his users loved the product, but he faced three big challenges.

First, most users loved the idea of the product, but once they started using it, they found it too difficult to use. They stayed for a few days and then disappeared. Entrepreneur Y had built the product for himself, was excited by all the users coming to his site, but was frustrated by the fact that he now served a new master: his users. They didn't require a lot of the advanced features he wanted to build. They wanted a product with fit and finish, a product that was polished and easy to use. They wanted someone to respond to their e-mail inquiries quickly when they had a question.

Second, his users didn't want to pay for the product—but he didn't want to display ads on the site.

The third challenge Entrepreneur Y faced was that he refused to change how the company made decisions. When the company was just a few of people, it worked reasonably well for everyone to participate in every decision. But as Entrepreneur Y added more engineers, the pace of change ground to a halt because decision making was too hard and time-consuming. Every employee in the company became Entrepreneur Y's boss.

A year later, his company was still in business, but users were struggling with the same product issues while the company struggled to put out a new release. Entrepreneur Y had always wanted to work for himself—right up until the moment he realized that wasn't as easy a prospect as he'd imagined it to be.

Friction Leads to Failure

Many people and their careers suffer from *drag*—friction that slows them down. This is the intangible sense that something isn't quite right, but they aren't sure what. Friction at work bleeds into other areas of your life, decreasing your overall happiness and productivity. You only appreciate how much after you begin working on something you really enjoy. As Steve Jobs said in his famous Stanford graduation speech, "Don't settle."

Everyone has bad days. But doing unfulfilling work week after week or year after year drags you down and prevents you from achieving your potential. That seems obvious, but according to a survey by the Conference Board research group, in 2009, only 45% of Americans were satisfied with their jobs. What's more, that satisfaction level has been declining for decades.

Investors are fond of analyzing the motivations and aspirations of entrepreneurs. Venture investors want to believe that an entrepreneur has the aspiration to build a billion-dollar (or bigger) company. But the only thing that really matters is your personal aspiration.

Being an entrepreneur is one of the most fulfilling ways you can spend your life. According to Professor of Entrepreneurial Studies Scott Shane at Case Western Reserve University, research indicates that "you would have to pay an entrepreneur 2.5 times as much for that person to have the same job satisfaction as an employee that he or she has as an entrepreneur."[1]

Bridge the Value Chasm

The *value chasm* is the difficult challenge that founders and CEOs face when deciding whether to hold or sell. Is it worth the significant additional risk, time, and ownership dilution (due to added capital) required to grow the business, or is it better to sell, make potentially life-changing money, and move on? To use the language of financial advisors, on a risk-adjusted basis, it makes more financial sense to sell.

Imagine you're an entrepreneur who has been working on your business for three years. You and your two co-founders each own 20% of the company. You've raised $5 million in venture capital. You have the option to sell today for $50 million in cash. To keep things simple, assume $5 million goes to your investors first, and the rest is divided up according to ownership. So, you get 20 percent of $45 million, or $9 million, before taxes.

Suppose that your alternative is to raise another $95 million and invest another 7 years building the business. After raising the $100M total, you and your co-founders are left with 5% ownership each. At the end of 10 years, to

---

[1] According to "Why Do People Become Entrepreneurs?" a post by Scott Shane, January 12, 2009. Shane is a professor of entrepreneurial studies at Case Western Reserve University. http://money.usnews.com/money/blogs/outside-voices-small-business/2009/01/12/why-do-people-become-entrepreneurs.

make the same amount of money, using the same math, your company must be worth $280 million, not taking into account the time value of money.[2] What's more, during the 7 years, you have to take the risk that the $9M you could have taken off the table may go to zero as the market changes, your company evolves, or your ownership stake is diluted. Plus, who knows what else you could do during those seven years? Perhaps you could build something even more valuable or impactful.

On a risk-adjusted basis, from a purely financial perspective, it makes more sense to sell. Granted, you're giving up the opportunity to make even more money if your company goes on to become worth billions. But by selling, you're taking potentially life-changing money off the table.

Starting a company isn't an inherently rational exercise! You have to be more than a little crazy to start a company, given the odds, challenges, and alternatives. You must, as one investor friend of mine likes to put it, "suspend disbelief."

That's why, when entrepreneurs and CEOs ask me for input on whether they should hold or sell, I tell them it's an intensely personal decision. It all comes back to your motivation and aspiration, to the heart of why you decided to become an entrepreneur to begin with—to run your own company, to change the world, and to realize your vision.

Personal Health

No book on startup failure would be complete without at least a few words on entrepreneur health. At my first startup, we had what we referred to as "the startup diet." This entailed ordering in pizza or grabbing takeout night after night, working out rarely if ever, and getting minimal sleep. Our poor health management took a toll in terms of both our personal health and productivity. We would find ourselves in meetings too exhausted to be productive.

Entrepreneur health deteriorates physically, emotionally, and psychologically. Long hours, constant stress, and poor dietary and sleep habits will wear anyone down. It may not seem as though taking time out for a run, gym session,

---

[2] The time value of money takes into account how much that money would have been worth had you been able to invest it over the same period of time—in this case, the cost of not having been paid the $9M seven years earlier, which you could have then invested to make more money.

or walk is the best use of time when customers are e-mailing, the phone is ringing off the hook, and a product update needs to be deployed.

But taking time out—even briefly—for physical and psychological fitness is critical to startup success. Not only do you end up feeling good, but a clear mind also leads you to better insights and better decisions. As legendary mountaineer Lou Whittaker once put it, investing in health and fitness is like making a deposit at the bank—you have to do it early so you can withdraw later when you need it.

Ways to Avoid Failure

This book has explored many of the reasons for startup failure. In the process, you've gone from taking the big leap, to building a great product and finding product-market fit, to scaling your company.

As you think about taking the leap or try to figure out how to change so you can scale your company after having been at it for a few years, here are some of the key questions to ask yourself.

Do You Deeply Understand Your Target Market?

Your target market can be yourself—especially if you're building a consumer product—or it can be a specific industry if you're building a business-to-business (B2B) product. Of course, one of the great appeals of building a consumer product is that you know the target market intimately!

If you're building a B2B product, you must know the target market equally well—either because you've come from the industry or because you've studied it. Often, coming from outside the industry makes it easier to be disruptive and transformative. But that means you need to understand the existing market limitations, customer requirements, and ecosystem.

Lots of entrepreneurs have failed because they didn't understand their markets. Some could never get traction because gorillas—behemoths who had been around for years—stood in their way, and they failed to find ways to disrupt them. The entrepreneurs didn't understand the strengths and weaknesses of existing players, both from a product and a go-to-market standpoint. Others never figured out what would make their product a must-have.

How Large Is the Market?

You may be perfectly happy building a product for a market of one—yourself. But if you want to have a bigger impact, need to generate revenue (directly or through a liquidity event), or both, this question matters.

For consumer Internet companies, the market is, by nature, big—potentially every person on Earth. The challenge is building something a very large number of people want and then reaching them. Consumer companies tend to be binary—lots of people love the product, or they don't.

For B2B companies, market evaluation and segmentation matter much more. It's easy to throw around big numbers, but the reality is that in a big market you have to start somewhere specific. "We're going to disrupt a $20B market" is a nice concept, but it's not actionable. You need to have specific segments in mind and understand them in detail.

Can You Reach the Market Efficiently?

Or, put another way, "What's your go-to-market strategy?" As I've discussed, in the end it all comes down to profitable acquisition and retention.

You may have a big market, but if that market is millions of small businesses with limited budgets, for example, you must have a strategy for reaching them efficiently—unless you plan to knock on 10 million doors yourself!

Your approach can be purely viral or word of mouth—get existing users to recruit new ones. Or you can buy ads or hire a huge telesales force. Whatever the case, having a plan for how to reach the market is critical, as is a way to measure what's working and what's not.

Do You Control Your Destiny?

I have met with countless entrepreneurs who talked about needing just one big deal for their company to work. Often that deal is with another large company, typically one that already has an efficient way to reach the market. Those entrepreneurs end up waiting a very, very long time. Plus, those who do get the one big deal frequently end up so dependent on it that they have difficulty broadening and scaling their businesses.

Entrepreneur X spent months trying to having meetings with the executives at a key partner. He believed that eventually the big company would begin working with him. The partner's employees took meetings and picked his brain, but he never made any business progress.

Eventually, the partner inked a big distribution deal with another company—headed by a friend of the partner's CEO. Entrepreneur X was incredulous. But to his credit, after recovering from his surprise, he admitted that the partner wasn't going to establish a business relationship with his company any time soon. He changed his distribution strategy. Had he not done so, his company would have gone out of business.

Do You Have Product Vision?

Some entrepreneurs start out with a product vision and then, when they realize no one wants their product, they fold like cheap lawn chairs. Some companies lose their product vision when their founders leave or are fired. You can hire for almost every other function—but not product vision.

Can You Build a Great Product?

Many products fail because they're terrible. They're designed poorly. They're too hard to use. They break. They're not self-explanatory. They're so complex that they're difficult to build and maintain.

Fortunately, today it's easy to get user feedback on your product. Internet services exist that for a few bucks let you have a user try your product and provide recorded feedback as they do so. There is nothing like seeing someone else try to use a product you've built. Over time, we all find workarounds for little things that don't work in our own products. But new users don't. They're honest about their product experience—and watching them use your product will cause you to be honest with yourself. Have strong opinions about what makes products great. Use those products, and internalize what you love about them.

Are You Relentless in Your Pursuit of Product-Market Fit?

This means not spending money, not scaling up, and not growing your organization and getting set on a certain path until you have product-market fit. If you're three or four years into building your company and things seem to be stagnant, chances are you don't have product-market fit. You may have some users, but you haven't found a big market that *must have* your product.

If you've turned over your management team several times and still aren't growing the way you want to, there's a chance it could be execution failure. But it's more likely a lack of product-market fit. Impatience is often an asset for startups—but not when it comes to scaling before you have product-market fit. Find product-fit before all else.

Can You Execute?

A lot of people have ideas for what they want to build. Few turn those into reality. Most people fail to get started. Of those who do begin, many grow bored or frustrated with the details required to succeed.

Executing means building. It means recruiting a team, putting together enough capital to build something, and selling your vision to others. It means scaling up personally and organizationally as your company grows. It means a relentless focus on delighting users and customers. It means not losing sight of product greatness even as sales, marketing, and finance become bigger and bigger parts of your business.

Are You Persistent?

When I talk with investors about the common characteristics that make up winning companies, time and again I hear, "great teams." When I press on what makes a great team, I consistently hear two things. First, great teams find great markets. And second, even—or especially—in the face of great adversity, problems, and challenges, great teams are persistent in their quest for success.

Are You Willing to Change Your Mind?

At the same time, the art of being an entrepreneur is all about having a thesis, testing that thesis, and then being willing to change your mind if your thesis is wrong. Persistence is critical to entrepreneurial success, but stubbornness can kill you. Finding the balance is what makes entrepreneurship an art, not a science.

Are You Crazy?

If your answer to this is "No way," then you're not an entrepreneur. I don't mean crazy in a bad way—I mean crazy enough to start a company, to make decisions that fly in the face of modern economic theory about risk-adjusted returns, and to take actions that go against the herd and the common wisdom.

Do You Simplify??

Some people make things simpler, while others make them more complex. Great entrepreneurs simplify.

If you can't communicate simply and clearly, you can't recruit, raise capital, or sell. Simplification leads to the best visions, the best products, and the highest likelihood of success. If you often find yourself being misunderstood or coming out of meetings thinking you could have communicated better, get help.

Who's Your Mentor?

You don't always begin with a great mentor. Many outstanding entrepreneurs don't know great mentors—or even know what a great mentor looks like—when they're starting out. Mentors come in many different forms: other founders, investors, board members, business partners, and, of course, family, friends, and personal relationships.

The key is to keep your eyes open along the way and acquire and surround yourself with great mentors as you go along.

Fail Fast

Most startups fail. America, and Silicon Valley in particular, is one of the few places where taking risk—whether it results in success or failure—is looked on positively. Although history is often rewritten to make it look like a successful entrepreneur tried one thing and it worked from the get-go, most entrepreneurs try multiple ideas and products before they hit the right one. Put another way, they fail repeatedly until they succeed. The successful ones conserve capital and keep their organizations small until they find product-market fit. Then they scale.

Most entrepreneurs have come closer than they care to admit to bankruptcy due to lack of product-market fit, failure to execute, or lack of capital.

Time is limited. Get focused. Fail fast.

Summary

When you read in *TechCrunch*, *VentureBeat*, and other news outlets about start-ups raising hundreds of millions of dollars at multi-billion dollar valuations, founders cashing out millions before their companies are acquired or go public, and companies getting to tens of millions of paying users in just a few years, keep in mind that this represents a very small minority of all startups.

The reality is that building a company from nothing into something valuable is a marathon, not a sprint. During that marathon, a lot can go wrong—product challenges, market changes, and team issues. Fortunately, America, and Silicon Valley in particular, smiles on risk raking, rather than frowning on it. By learning from the lessons in this book, you can avoid the key causes of failure and lead your startup to success.

Index

CPSIA information can be obtained at www.ICGtesting.com
Printed in the USA
LVOW121632310112

266405LV00005B/163/P